Expecting the Good

Inspiration From a Badass with a Big Heart

By

Brigitte Cutshall

© Copyright 2018 Brigitte Cutshall

First Edition

July 2018 – 1st printing
October 2018—2nd printing
July 2019—3rd printing

Library of Congress Control Number: 2018906262
ISBN: 978-0-9787475-4-1 (soft-cover version)
ISBN: 978-0-9787475-5-8 (eBook version)

Published by Gemini Media, Inc.
Acworth, GA

Editor: Megan Copenhaver and Michele Downey
Cover Design: Tracy Stalling

A definition of "good"

Having the qualities to be desired or approved of; helps define moral behavior, cultural values, and what kind of beliefs we teach our children.

Dedicated to Jean-Luc

Table of Contents

Foreword — 9

Introduction — 13
    The Intrapraneur
    Take Responsibility for Who You Choose to Be
    A Silent Leader

The Long Gray Line — 25
    The West Point Tour
    The Unexpected Audio
    Classmate Stories

The Challenge — 60
    The Family Life
    Meeting the Family
    The Meetup
    An Unexpected Departure
    Operation Urgent Fury
        Harry Shaw's Story
        Tim's Perspective
    Defense Language Institute
    The Cross Country Adventure
    For the Love of Skiing

The Africa Tour — 101
    Sudan
    Psychological Operations
    Operation Desert Storm
    Defense Attaché Course
    Chad
    Back "Home" Again

The Civilian Life — 125
    The Grandpa Role
    9-11
    Florida: the Final Destination
    A Grandson's Tribute

Epilogue — 146
    Letter to a Grandson
    Final Thoughts

Acknowledgements — 151

Foreword

The last time I saw Jean-Luc Nash was at our 40th West Point graduation anniversary in 2015. It was unbelievable to be all together again on that campus. We had plans to reconnect later but Jean-Luc passed away in March 2016 before that could happen.

At the time of my retirement in September 2013, after 38 years of active duty, I was the oldest serving Green Beret on active duty at 60 years old. I didn't really think too much about that. Then my son gave me a leather-bound book at retirement – it was full of blank pages. "Dad, you never talk about what you did in the military. Would you please, at some point, write down some of the things that you've done."

Jean-Luc and I were both very aware and sensitive to the fact that as part of our duty, in defense of the nation, we had to be careful with what information was shared.

I'm participating in this book because I know that Jean-Luc would want me to help his daughter out and would be supportive. It's an honor actually. Jean-Luc was very positive in most situations and liked to focus on the good.

We believed in what we did and what we were trained to do in service to our nation. The heroes of our country were our precious families. Our families carried on with life, never knowing if they'd ever see us again, never knowing truly what we were doing. We spent our adult lives protecting the families of the world at the expense of our own.

It's normal that families learn what their military family members did in uniform from those they served with rather than from the individual. Understand that it's hard for a soldier to reintegrate into their family after being away so much.

These are examples of normal life experiences and challenges we deal with. When my father died, I was deployed; and when my son was diagnosed with cancer, I was deployed. When my wife had open heart surgery, people felt sorry for me. I told others that I was happy to be with my family during that time. To be at home with my family during that experience was a blessing.

Then I had my open heart surgery, a triple bypass. Compared to my other near-death experiences, I liked that one the best. People look at me like I'm crazy when I say that and ask - Why? Because it's an experience I can share with my family. The other near-death experiences I can't talk about or I won't talk about. Not only can I share that surgery experience with others, but my wife now has a frame of reference because she had a similar surgery.

What I admire most about Jean-Luc is that he displayed a consistent level of courage on a daily basis. Moral courage, emotional courage, physical courage. He was able to always do the right thing, for the right reason; whether anybody else saw it, whether anybody else would do it, or if anybody else would recognize it. It didn't make a difference if anyone else would appreciate it. He didn't worry about that.

Jean-Luc and I were a tag-team, we knew that what we were doing was the right thing. It was the right thing because we were being honest, we were being candid, and we were being transparent. We also recognized our frailties as human beings.

The physical courage that I witnessed Jean-Luc perform by my side, and often for me, was profound. It bound us together. Even though we went our separate ways in the Special Forces community, and we literally went to different parts of the world, we stayed connected because we selected the most challenging duty assignments.

These assignments needed to be done and they needed to be done well. We were willing to do that for our nation.

To do those tasks in another culture, and to be surrounded by people from a different culture that spoke a different language and did things differently, was very difficult.

I did it in Nicaragua, El Salvador, Haiti, Iraq, Kosovo, and in Afghanistan. Jean-Luc was in Korea on his first Special Forces assignment and later in Africa. He took it a step further and did it as a contractor after retirement from active duty. I never did that because I had the privilege to continue to serve on active duty.

Being in a Special Forces advisory role is physically and emotionally demanding. You are constantly surrounded by people you really don't understand and what motivates them. You can speak the language and have an insight into a different culture, but you really don't understand the underlying motivation or if you can trust them.

We all want our family to be proud of us and establish a personal example of trying to be a good human being. We want to always do the right thing. Some people think – gee, I don't know what the right thing to do is. That's not accurate. We all know deep down what the right thing to do is in any given situation. In that situation, do you have the courage and the conviction to accept the consequences of doing the right thing?

Making a decision to do the right thing when it's physically dangerous is difficult. Doing the right thing even if you might get fired because someone else is not as honorable as you are, is difficult. Be a good person and do the right thing.

Know how precious and uncertain life is.

Keith M. Huber, Lieutenant General, US Army (retired)

Keith speaks on leadership and ethics on a regular basis. He has an office at Middle Tennessee State University and serves as a Senior Advisor for Veterans and Leadership initiatives.

Introduction

You know it's probably not a good thing when the phone rings at 1:30am.

It was a Saturday night (technically Sunday morning) when I received one of those calls while in bed. After waking up from the abrupt phone call, my initial panicked thoughts were that one of my sons was in a car accident or had been arrested.

A Florida phone number was displayed and my thoughts turned to "Oh My God!" something happened to mom and Jean-Luc is calling! My heart started pounding immediately.

It was the opposite. My mom was the person on the other line, calling from the hospital and with unexpected news. My stepfather, Jean-Luc, had just died from a massive heart attack. It happened while he was working out earlier at home in his basement gym. She heard a big crash and checked it out. He was unresponsive, she immediately called 911 and started CPR.

My mom was obviously in shock, yet, calmly asked me to call my brother and sister with the news. I called them immediately and tried to remain as calm as our mother.

How can this happen to a *healthy* and vibrant person? In reality we're all going to die, but our expectation was that it would be my mom first; she thought so as well. Jean-Luc was 64 years old and younger than our mother.

Less than a week later, we were all gathered at their church for the funeral services. This was surreal. My Uncle Claude and cousin, Matthieu, flew in from France. The church was filled with many people that came to pay their last respects to Jean-Luc—family, friends, neighbors, and church members. About 15 of his West Point classmates attended and there was a Special Forces memorial for him at the NAS (Naval Air Station) cemetery.

His West Point buds held a "Benny's Wake" for him later that evening at the hotel they were staying at. The West Pointers told my family that a Benny's Wake is a time to recall a personal story and to publicly share with others; the majority of the stories were funny. We learned so much about him through the eyes of his fellow cadets.

Everyone needed this laughter and their stories reminded us all why Jean-Luc made everyone smile. He embraced the chaos of the moment and brought out the best in others.

We tend to assume we have total control our lives and there is order to every day. We stick to our routines and our habits, yet at any moment it can be disrupted just when we thought everything was all planned out. Every person has at least one story to demonstrate that life doesn't always go as intended.

We eventually develop an appreciation for life by seeing and experiencing its frailty. Death is part of life. Death is also a reminder not to take things in your life for granted and live while you can.

Jean-Luc was one of my main influencers at a very critical point in my life. He gave me a chance and the actual opportunity to succeed. If it wasn't for his generosity, who really knows where I'd be at today.

My only regret is I never acknowledged this with him in person. But he knew.

Jean-Luc witnessed a lot of global suffering by civilians through his work with the military and time as an international consultant. Because of his own experiences, he focused a lot on his grandchildren to make sure the next generation was prepared to handle what comes their way in life.

"Things that are unsaid stay with us forever. Then one day we're gone." We have all these things to say and this is why I decided to write about my stepfather.

The Intrapreneur

It was a Friday evening in early October. My sister and I were staying at my friend Angela's house for the weekend while our father was deer hunting with some hunting buddies; then there was a knock on the front door. Angela's mother answered and she had to call my name a few times to get my attention.

Angela and I were listening to music and had the music blasting. This was the beginning of the MTV era and videos... we were mesmerized.

I was surprised to see my mom standing behind this tall guy on the front porch. He introduced himself to me politely "Hi, my name is Jean-Luc. Nice to meet you." I really don't remember our verbal exchange, but do remember being a little annoyed about the situation. Oh great, a military guy.

I had this perception that military guys were chauvinistic; partly because I grew up near Fort Benning, and my father told me to stay far away from military guys because they did not have the best intentions for young girls like me. He was retired from the Army, a Vietnam veteran, and I believed him.

My demeanor in the beginning after Jean-Luc met my mother probably wasn't the best. The knock on Angela's front door was about three months after my parent's divorce was finalized, from the father that adopted me and my brother; this was my sister's biological father.

Jean-Luc wasn't overwhelmed with the family situation because he viewed it as a challenge that could be overcome. He could be stern and came across as being an ass sometimes when I was younger; most likely I was being an ass with a bad teen attitude and opinionated. I hadn't learned to filter myself yet and was trying to grasp having another man around my mother.

Over the years, my worldview of men changed after seeing how Jean-Luc treated our mother. He treated her with a lot of respect and encouraged her to pursue her dreams. "Don't let any excuses hold you back or get in the way" is what he always told her. He did the same with all of us.

Despite my attitude in the beginning, Jean-Luc also took care of me for a brief time during that critical transition from high school to college, and he raised my sister from the age of 11. It's kind of funny that he went from being a single guy, never married, to being a father to three children and two of them were girls. His Special Forces training came in handy maybe?

Mom credits Jean-Luc for making her a better person. Her exact words to me after his death were "I was jaded about life until I met Jean-Luc. He showed me that life was worth living."

He definitely became the glue that bound our family together. This provided some 'normalcy' for us all.

Jean-Luc reminds me of an intrapreneur with his approach to our family. His purpose in my family's situation was to improve the relationship we had with our mother. We were skeptical at first because this was our mother's 3rd marriage right after I turned 17. And their marriage lasted 33 years!

What is exactly is an intrapreneur? An intrapreneur is someone who innovates within an existing system that they didn't build, driven by a larger purpose, and drawn to connect with others to form a network. Intrapreneurs have a vision and see the world as it can be. They don't spend energy complaining about the status quo or chipping away at changing it.

Jean-Luc was someone who stood out in a crowd. He was tall, athletic, and had a distinctive posture that seemed to sway or lean to the right. This was most noticeable when he paused to talk with others.

JL appears to be giving some advice to my younger son. Seeing this picture again gave me the idea to write a book about him.

There seemed to always be a slight grin on his face as he was listening, and didn't come across as stern or rigid with others. His persona was trustworthy and people felt comfortable asking and receiving his advice. He wasn't afraid to have difficult conversations either.

Jean-Luc really enjoyed to tell stories; especially to all the grandkids because they admired him and were a captive audience. Each story was full of intrigue that kept them engaged. He could take a random fact and turn it into an adventure. They all enjoyed spending time with him and all the grandsons referred to him as "Bad-Ass Grandpa."

Writing a book would have been a perfect outlet for him. I'm not sure he would agree with me but I wish he would have shared more of his experiences before his unexpected death.

I want to acknowledge that writing this book also will help to better understand the impact being part of the military can have on people. They can positively affect others through their leadership by expecting the good in others. That's my assertion anyway.

JL was not a procrastinator and was strong at planning; that can be attributed to his military and diplomat experiences. My siblings and I joked how methodical he was in planning family trips, even a simple trip to the grocery store.

He always gave us the departure time as if we were on a military assignment..."*Guys, we are leaving at 0-900 tomorrow*" rather than stating we are leaving at 9am. This also meant your butt better be ready *before* 0-900.

Jean-Luc was a man of honor and very generous. He was not perfect - as no human is - but everyone could count on him to do the right thing, be there for his country and his family. JL was clear with his expectations with everyone in each role he was a part of. That is a major contributing factor to his overall success in life.

We noticed a big change in him after his retirement. He was more at ease overall. Maybe he didn't change but was simply able to spend more time with the family finally, no more long-term international gigs to deal with. His main goal became to help prepare his grandchildren to handle life better.

Take Responsibility for Who You Choose to Be

When you blame others, you give up the power to change. ~Unknown

That was one of Jean-Luc's favorite sayings...*take responsibility for who you choose to be.* He was not quick to judge or react negatively. He developed an appreciation for the meaning of life by acknowledging its imperfections and he always emphasized the positive aspect with us.

JL also emphasized that there are problems all around us that we don't have any control over but we need to take responsibility for our choices. He was the living example.

So what do you really have control over?

That's a question Jean-Luc recommended that we ask ourselves every day. It's a simple reminder that how you choose to act (or react) and present yourself is in your control. His ability to remain calm in any situation is a reflection of this.

People tend to put too much energy into what they can't control. This ends up creating anxiety and can affect your health and relationships in the long run. It's best to put your energy into smaller things where you can influence the outcome. Each small step will build upon another, which allows change to happen over time.

Being responsible demonstrates how effectively you're managing your life when an opportunity to make a choice presents itself. When that responsible moment comes, what you do or don't do is a choice, and is an indication of the type of person you really are.

Everyone can be impulsive sometimes, make mistakes and make poor choices. *Personal* responsibility is taking ownership of your own behavior and the consequences that follow. It can be difficult to have self-respect or respect for others unless you take responsibility for your actions. Jean-Luc did not blame others for his behavior and was a great example of taking responsibility.

Part of personal responsibility is to also acknowledge what you don't know. Recognize you need input from others sometimes because you really don't know everything. Be open to learning because learning never ends. Find interesting and meaningful things to do and be involved with. This is how you grow and change. JL definitely emphasized the importance of learning new things.

Indirect responsibility is taking action to help others or situations around you. It's not the same level of being personally responsible, but you get to choose whether to get involved and help...or not. If you do decide to get involved, be kind with others, including any feedback that you give or receive.

Life can be better overall when you take responsibility for your own actions. My choice? I will do the best I can with this life, put my energy to good use and create impactful work ... just like Jean-Luc.

A Silent Leader

The first response in a situation reveals who you truly are.

One of Jean-Luc's best traits was his curiosity and was not quick to pass any judgement. A silent leader is probably the most succinct way to describe Jean-Luc.

Many of us have (or had) silent leaders in our lives and one of mine was Jean-Luc. They have a powerful impact because you really don't have to say much to be a great leader. And when they do lead, others tend to follow just because of who they are.

My stepfather remained calm in every aspect of his life. My husband is the same way and doesn't react. Each situation is assessed in a quiet and silent manner before making a decision and then responding. I attribute that to their military training.

"Silent" is probably not a word you normally expect to be associated with great leadership. There's nothing shy or passive about silent leaders and these types of leaders are just as effective as the more outspoken ones. Silent leaders utilize their influence through action over words.

Jean-Luc had an overall "quiet" confidence rather than arrogance or driven by ego. He wasn't necessarily introverted but preferred to solve problems through collaboration, logical thought and encouragement rather than relying on aggression or dominance.

Here are a few more examples of what a silent leader like JL can entail:

- They are compassionate, understanding, open and approachable. Most importantly, they have earned respect rather than lead through force of character.

- They show by example and know they can't expect others to do anything they aren't willing to do themselves. It starts with them and they set the example. They take the initiative and determine how they're going to act in any given situation before the situation arises.

- They follow through on their commitments. They have the drive and have mastered the ability to do what they say they'll do and always finish.

- They continuously teach through their actions and beliefs that correspond with the words they say. They also aren't the type to nag you or micromanage others. Actions are the biggest teachers.

- They show their humility in their accomplishments and understand that any accomplishment isn't achieved without help from others. And when they fail, they are willing to take critical feedback and make changes that are necessary.

Like everyone, I've made mistakes and some "interesting" decisions, yet Jean-Luc didn't yell or scorn me for it. He would calmly ask "what did you learn" and "what could be different next time?" It all has a way of working out.

The Long Gray Line

The simplest interpretation of the phrase *The Long Gray Line* is a continuum of all graduates and cadets of West Point, USMA (United States Military Academy). It's a brotherhood so to speak. I heard Jean-Luc mention that phrase a few times but didn't really question the meaning.

Jean-Luc's character was formed by being a part of the *Long Gray Line.* This connection to West Point gave him a sense of meaning in life.

Jean-Luc with his father, Gerald, at West Point

The military is a relevant part of our society with a purpose to defend our country and protect us from unexpected dangers. The military is now also expected to defend and help advance

U.S. values, interests, and objectives. This is something many people take for granted and don't appreciate, including myself even though it was the environment I grew up around.

Why join the military? What's the attraction? Every person has a different reason. The most common reason lies around gaining skills and training (and education) for "free." It also gives many people a purpose in life, a sense of meaning, and renews their hope for a better future. It also provides a group identity that you can be a part of.

Having a sense of meaning in life and belonging to something greater than oneself is worth a lot more than most people realize. Having "meaning" comes from helping others in small or big ways and making a positive impact.

Many of us have family members that have served in the military; or you at least know someone who has served others in some capacity, including police officers, firemen, etc. It can be a valuable experience that many choose to take.

I asked two of Jean-Luc's fellow West Point classmates, Dan Alexander and Stan Moore, about their perspective of *The Long Gray Line*.

Dan Alexander, Colonel, US Army (retired)

"The Long Gray Line means everything to a graduate of West Point for it embodies everyone and everything we believe in and are taught at United States Military Academy (USMA).

The Long Gray Line stands for all of the graduates who have ever called themselves West Pointers, worn the ring with honor and distinction, and served by the strictest code of Duty, Honor, Country -- some 68,000 at last count. The USMA cadets are probationary members of the Long Gray Line.

The Long Gray Line persona reflects the cultural beliefs that we hold so close to our hearts those of Duty, Honor, Country. Just thinking about The Long Gray Line brings tears to my eyes and pounding to my heart and "a thrill that its presence imparts." I can trust any member of The Long Gray Line to come to my aid in times of trouble without hesitation.

In the alma mater the Long Gray Line is further defined: "The Long Gray Line of us stretches through the years of the centuries told and the last man feels to his marrow the grip of this far off hold." Every graduate knows that if he defiles in battle the code of the Long Gray Line he defiles the ghosts of the tens of thousands of graduates who have died before him.

That's probably a major reason why you never find any academy graduates on charges of cowardice in battle; we would rather die first. For me it was the knowledge of The Long Gray Line praying for me during and after my Widow-maker heart attack that helped me maintain my will to live at my darkest moment.

We can always count on The Long Gray Line to "Grip hands tho it be from the shadows as we swear as we did of yore For living or dying to honor the Corps and the Corps and the Corps."

Dan has a mural of *The Long Gray Line* hanging on the wall in his living room as a reminder and "as testimony to my belief in the Long Gray Line to do what's right when My country needs us most."

Stan Moore, Lieutenant Colonel, US Army (retired)

"The Long Gray Line. I am not sure how the term originated. It is used in the words of two well-known old West Point songs, included below.

I still have an attachment to the old school. It remains a very unusual place, almost Old European in its appearance. I was last there in 2014, when I was invited to do a 12 mile road march with the New Cadets as they moved from field training back to West Point. One of my friends lives just outside the gate, and his family has been attending the school for 7 generations!

When Jean-Luc and I attended, it was brutally difficult, especially the first year. I wanted to quit, but my pride and stubbornness would not let me.

I have come to appreciate West Point more as I age. It gave me good training and provided me a huge number of opportunities."

Hail Alma Mater dear,
To us be ever near.
Help us thy motto bear
Through all the years.
Let Duty be well performed.
Honor be e'er untarned.
Country be ever armed.
West Point, by thee.
Guide us, thy sons, aright,
Teach us by day, by night,
To keep thine honor bright,
For thee to fight.
When we depart from thee,
Serving on land or sea,
May we still loyal be,
West Point, to thee.
And when our work is done,
Our course on earth is run,
May it be said, "Well done;
Be thou at peace."
E'er may that line of gray
Increase from day to day
Live, serve, and die, we pray,
West Point, for thee.
P.S. Reinecke, 1911

This song "The Corp" best expresses the sentiment of *The Long Gray Line*.

The Corps! Bareheaded salute it,
With eyes up, thanking our God --
That we of the Corps are treading
Where they of the Corps have trod --
They are here in ghostly assemblage,
the men of the Corps long dead,
And our hearts are standing attention
While we wait for the passing tread.
We, sons of to-day, we salute you --
You, sons of an earlier day;
We follow, close order, behind you,
Where you have pointed the way;
The long gray line of us stretches
Thro' the years of a century told,
And the last man feels to his marrow
The grip of your far off hold.
Grip hands with us now, though we see not,
Grip hands with us, strengthen our hearts
As the long line stiffens and straightens
With the thrill that you presence imparts.
Grips hands tho' it be from the shadows --
While we swear, as you did of yore,
Or living, or dying, to honor
The Corps, and the Corps, and the Corps!
The Late Bishop H.S. Shipman

The West Point Tour

West Point has been inspiring, educating and training those of character with leadership skills for over 200 years. Getting accepted into an institution such as West Point is a remarkable accomplishment in itself.

West Point was referenced a lot by my stepfather, Jean-Luc, and how much that experience meant to him because it definitely affected his worldview. It helped Jean-Luc determine what his purpose was in life and he stayed on that path to help others.

I really wanted to visit West Point in person ... the institution that shaped JL's life, his perceptions, his opportunities. Did his experience there change his personality in at all? I viewed him as a realist. Is that true? It's my perception of him anyway. He accepted any situation and was prepared to deal with it.

My visit and personal tour of West Point was prompted by an unexpected email. Captain Zachary Willey was referred to me by one of my clients. Zachary needed help with sourcing for a new training program he developed. He happens to be a 2009 West Point graduate and a West Point instructor as of this writing.

After a few email exchanges, he offered to help me in any way I needed. So of course I took him up on the offer. An unexpected and good outcome.

I didn't want to go alone and decided to ask my youngest son to go with me and he was definitely up for it. Before we entered the actual campus, my son and I checked out the museum to kill some time before Zachary could get us. That area was under construction for an updated Visitor Center.

Zachary picked us up in his personal car just outside the West Point entrance gate at McDonald's. I viewed that as a twist of satire - there is a McDonald's "golden arches" literally outside the security entrance of West Point with its own elaborate arched gateway.

The first thing I did when Zachary came up to us and said "Are you Brigitte?" was to give him a big "mom" hug. I don't know what compelled me to do so and it probably surprised him. I was so happy and grateful at the moment. My son shook his hand instead.

The campus is breathtaking because of its location on the Hudson River and surrounding architecture. It's hard to describe in a few simple words. And so much history in one location! During the visit, we were reminded that West Point was founded by George Washington.

The Hudson River view on campus

I believe that understanding the importance of history will help us all make better decisions. And a visit to West Point is highly recommended and something to put on your to-do list. There are a lot of books about West Point topics and trivia; but nothing compares to being there in person. Nothing.

There is about 1300 acres for cadet training. We only accessed the main part of the campus because of the time-frame allotted. The inside of the Chow Hall was massive and had awe-inspiring architecture. I understand now why my stepfather and those just like him stay connected to that place.

Zach mentioned that during his time there as a cadet for 4 years, you sat at the same table for each meal with cadets from different levels (plebes, etc). Food was passed around family style.

The Chow Hall

One requirement of being accepted into the academy is to participate in a sport. Academics and sports happen during the school year and combat training happens in the summer. There are multiple facilities on campus—a football field, soccer field, baseball field, track and field, basketball court, and a tennis court just to name a few. West Point even offers youth summer camps each year for multiple sports.

We were impressed with the ice hockey rink. The building is set on a hill, seemed like on a cliff actually, and was very steep to get to and from the parking lot. My son felt at home at the rink because he played travel hockey for many years and stopped playing before his first year of college. I'm sure Grandpa was smiling down at us.

Zachary's generosity with me is an example of a West Point graduate, *The Long Gray Line*, whose character and leadership skills were honed to help others. He certainly didn't hesitate to help Jean-Luc's daughter.

The Unexpected Audio

Jean-Luc's roommate at West Point, Don Mooney, shared an audio interview of JL. It was so cool to hear JL's voice sharing some funny stories of his time at West Point. It actually made me tear up. The interview occurred in the late summer of 2015, about 9 months before his death.

Don is a 'people person' and very honest by JL's description. They both have this unique ability to connect with others and are very determined. They can be laser focused and make it happen, whatever they're trying to attain. This is probably an attribute of their West Point training.

Jean-Luc started off explaining that West Point is set up in a Regimental format, with 4 different Regiments. He mentioned that the 1st Regiment had a very stern reputation, they were 'hard asses.' The 4th Regiment had a reputation of being more fun and looser. Can you guess which regiment they were in? JL and Don were in the same company and were assigned to D4.

In JL's interview he emphasized the importance of the Mess Hall (some call it the Chow Hall). There are unique traditions to dining there that are developed by the cadet companies. He didn't get into specific traditions for his company.

Jean-Luc and Don each had a bit of a rebel streak in them apparently. JL mentioned the West Point Honor Code is *Don't Lie, Steal, or Tolerate Those That Do*. JL then continues to state "that doesn't mean you can't break the rules; if you happen to get caught, just don't lie about it."

Don had a tendency to get caught when he broke a rule.

His biggest infraction had him confined to the campus for almost the last 2 years at West Point. As a Junior, you are not allowed to have a car. Apparently, Don did have a car but kept it off campus in a garage near Newburgh.

Don was caught when his girlfriend, Narcissa, had an accident outside the gate of Camp Buckner after visiting Don the summer before his Junior year. She was going to drive the car back to Newburgh for him but did not have a driver's license at the time. The car was registered in Don's name.

So Jean-Luc filled in and took Don's girlfriend out on dates - she was able to visit Don on campus - but JL took her to the clubs on a regular basis. He spent more time with Narcissa than Don did the last two years at West Point.

You are allowed to get a car your Senior sear. Don just did it too soon. And you can *never* get a motorcycle, it was frowned upon. Well it turns out Jean-Luc got a motorcycle his Senior year ... you'd think he would have been afraid to break a rule after being Don's roommate. That didn't stop him from getting a 500cc VSA Victor Special.

Jean-Luc described it as a classic British motorcycle which is code for not reliable. It broke down a lot in other words. The electronics didn't work and always had problems. He kept it off base but didn't mention where it was stored. So most times, he had to hitchhike back to West Point. Yet it was worth it to him because he got to ride around the state of New York on a motorcycle.

Hitchhiking became one of JL's favorite things to do since he didn't have reliable transportation. When Don was able to leave the campus, they would hitchhike together.

The first big hitchhiking expedition was to Houston, TX where Don is from, and they went there via Alabama.

The 2nd big hitchhiking adventure was to New York City. They got a partial ride back from two girls and were dropped off by a wall, near a bridge, that was actually part of a cemetery. It was dark and winter time, very cold. They found a moving truck that had some blankets inside; it wasn't locked obviously.

JL and Don decided to borrow the blankets and slept by a wall and didn't realize they were near a cemetery until the morning. When they woke up at dawn, they returned the blankets to the truck and hitchhiked back to West Point.

Another thing they liked to do was go to Clubs, specifically the club in Newburgh that was an all-black club. That ended when Don was in confinement. As mentioned before, JL would take Don's girlfriend out instead by himself and that included the Newburg club. One night they were dancing and some random guy came up to JL and Narcissa and stated "You can do better than that honkey."

There was a pause and JL replied "yes, she can" instead of punching him (which is what would have happened if Don and JL were together). Thankfully, nothing happened and they kept on dancing, enjoying themselves.

Richard Nixon came to visit the campus at one point. It's a tradition that when a President visits West Point, he will grant amnesty to all the cadets; particularly important to those in confinement. That's how Don got amnesty. To this day, Don actually likes Richard Nixon because the amnesty erased the confinement from his records.

Don learned his lesson about breaking the rules after that.

JL and Don graduated in 1975 which was also America's 200th birthday, an extra celebration for that class.

When you graduate from West Point, you get a 60 day break before your first military assignment. Don was engaged and planned to get married in that timeframe. But first, Don had to have a Bachelor party. The "bachelor party" basically consisted of Don and JL, and they decided to take a flight to Spain and hitchhike to Denmark to fly back. They didn't really think it through much, no planning involved.

Don told JL he could speak Spanish and would take care of getting around Spain and order food. And JL could speak French and would take care of that part. But Don didn't really know Spanish as much as he thought. Every meal in Spain was squid. No matter where they were, squid was included. *Side note, one of JL's favorite meals to order at a Thai restaurant with the family was squid salad.*

Hitchhiking was harder to do in Europe because they stood out - they were big Americans - and couldn't fit in a lot of the Euro vehicles. They got a little desperate at one point and hopped onto a flatbed truck that was parked at a restaurant and hid under some covers. The border guard in France did not notice them, thankfully, otherwise who knows what would have happened. Since they ended up in France, they stayed longer than expected there and visited with some of JL's relatives. They got out of France in a similar manner; hiding in the bed of a truck.

When they arrived in Switzerland, one of the first things they did was stop to eat at a Swiss restaurant that was advertised as 'all you can eat.' As Americans they ate way too much and were asked to leave.

Later on, they hitchhiked to Amsterdam and ended up at a Club. Some random guy came up to them and asked to look at JL's West Point ring. This guy also asked JL to take the ring off so he could hold it. Don responded "Don't you do that!"

JL ignored Don and took his ring off, handed it to this guy. Once the ring was in his hand, he tried to run off. A fight ensued. JL got his ring back. *I've learned that JL is very trusting of others and gives them a benefit of the doubt.*

This "bachelor party" ended up being 32 days in Europe. Since JL was the Best Man, he had to make sure the groom arrives for the wedding and they got back just in time.

Don mentioned at the Benny's Wake for JL (after his funeral) that as Best Man, Jean-Luc was responsible for the wedding rings. Guess what? JL forgot them and they had to drive to Narcissa's parents' house. All the doors were locked, so they climbed up the wall in their Dress Blues into an open window on the 2nd floor to gain access to the house. The rings were found!

They ended up back at the church with the rings - and a little sweaty and dusty. JL didn't mention forgetting the wedding rings in the interview I listened to.

"The military life takes you all over and separates you from close friends and family." These are Jean-Luc's exact words from the interview. Over the years he and Don kept in touch.

JL went to the Jump School Basic Course immediately after in Fort Benning, GA. Then he was stationed in Korea, Turkey and Germany where JL was a Special Forces officer.

Don was stationed in Germany too in the same timeframe and they were able to visit a few times over there. Then they didn't see each other again until after they both retired from the military. Don moved back to Houston. JL was in Florida.

JL considered Don to be his best friend; actually he has two best friends - Don and his wife, Narcissa. Jean-Luc didn't meet and marry my mother until 7 years after he graduated from West Point. He thought it was important that spouses connect, and was happy that my mom and Narcissa did.

Everyone has a different take on their shared experiences. There is a lot of information available about West Point and different topics. Zachary Willey recommended I locate the yearbook of their 1975 graduation. There is a quote for each graduate that encapsulates the experience there.

Don actually wrote Jean-Luc's yearbook quote and is a perfect description of him:

His faded blue jeans, grease-stained shirt only supplement the spirit of the "Easy Rider" who lived for adventure. Whether thumbing, climbing, cycling, or dreaming about it in class, Jean-Luc never let his mind stay here longer than necessary.

JEAN-LUC MARCEL NASH D-4
Fairbanks, Alaska

His faded blue jeans, grease-stained shirt only supplement the spirit of the "Easy Rider" who lived for adventure. Whether thumbing, climbing, cycling, or dreaming about it in class, John never let his mind stay here longer than necessary.

Behavioral Science Club 3, 2, 1; Karate 2, 1; Mountaineering Club 2, President 1; Riding Club 4, 3, 2, 1; Cadet Public Relations Council 3, 2.

LIEUTENANT

CLASS OF 1975
First Row: J. Ferrara, F. Caputo, M. Coletti, D. Green, D. Mooney. *Second Row:* D. Kelley, S. Johnson. *Third Row:* J. Mode, J. Wasiak, B. Quirk, L. Smith, G. Bishop, D. Alexander. *Fourth Row:* R. Richard, L. Kovar, C. Edwards, M. Genetti. *Fifth Row:* J. Nash, L. Jordan, M. Oscar, D. Pevoski. *Not Pictured:* B. Harris, D. Heine, S. Townes.

D-4

We entered West Point amidst the flash of lightning and the roar of thunder, symbols of the challenges which we were to encounter throughout our four years as cadets. Those four years were made bearable through the insanity of the party spirit which carried us through the gray of gloom, the knife point of LES, and the sleepless nights of TEE'S. During those four years the metamorphosis of 24 individuals into a single group with an undefeatable spirit was our answer to all challenges. The 1975 class of Delta Quad possessed a union of friendship that surprised us all.

Plebe year will be remembered for its Saturday mornings spent in the library, the wet, wet victory over Navy and the first snow a-la-mode. Yearling year found us as the happy wanderers — each going his own way. This was the year that we lost a few. The remainder were growing steadily stronger. Cow year was our year to regroup and reorganize. Bear Mountain Inn saw us as a group on 500th night and Camelot learned the "Bump" during Ring Weekend.

Our last year has been the culmination of a steady unification of spirit. Coffee call removed the pain of day-to-day routine, and Saturday Buffets found us removing all the pain. The quotes that stood for Delta Quad were: "If you ain't tap dancing!", "Typically Nasty Weather", "Who do?", "You Do!", "Lou who!", "That's lite", "Oh Baby, Oh Wow.", "A wed, wed nose", "Turkey of the Week is . . ." In conclusion it was parties, parties, parties. "It's twue, it's twue," that this was the Quad: Alex, Chief, Paisan (little wop), Caputs, Claybird, Moondog, Polack (Pevosk)(ski), Waz, Fraz (PJ), Genets (Big Wop), Green Jeans (Greener), Hooker, Heindog, Gnasher (Ranger, Jeanluck, and Poor Devil), CC Quirk, Scottie (Mr. Bad), Lance, Lord Kelley (amigo), The Shoe (Kojak), Modo, "O", Virge, Smitty, Steven Delta Townes.

Classmate Stories

After Jean-Luc's death, I wanted to learn more about him before he met our mother. I reached out to some of his fellow West Pointers and asked if they had any stories to share.

D-4 Beanheads 1971

Don Mooney, Lieutenant Colonel, US Army (retired)

Here is an excerpt from Don's "Benny's Wake" speech.

"I would generally say that Jean-Luc was my brother. The last text he sent me - he signed it "brother." He was the Best Man at my wedding, he was the Best Man literally.

He had a great effect on people, and he's one of the reasons why I married this woman right next to me. You know guys, I was a stellar cadet (laughter).

I never got into trouble until I met Narcissa. Jean-Luc probably went out with her as much as I did, because I was in confinement. I was confined to my room and was confined to West Point, and couldn't take her off post.

When I was getting ready to graduate, Jean-Luc asked me "Don, what are you going to do with Narcissa?" I said I was going to love her and leave her. He said to me "You know she's smarter than you." (Laughter) - Those were his exact words. And so I consequently went and proposed to her.

On our wedding day - again he was our best man - he was supposed to have the wedding rings. We are in our Dress Blues. The preacher asks for the rings. Where are the rings? Well, Jean-Luc had left them back at the house. So we had to rush back to Narcissa's house, climb to the 2nd floor in our Dress Blues, and get the rings.

Anyway, Jean-Luc was quite a man. I know that we all love him, and that's why we're here. He was my best friend, my best man, and my brother."

Joseph Wasiak, Colonel, US Army (retired)

"Friends of mine from years ago would be surprised to hear me say that I think cars are overrated; way overrated. Considering I spent the majority of my Firstie year rebuilding a car in a garage in Vails Gate not far from West Point, that statement just doesn't make sense. But I never really did get excited about cars, they were always just means of transportation and not much more. Unless of course, we're talking about British sports cars, especially old British sports cars. MG T Series & A's, Triumph TR6s, Morgans, Austin Healy 3000s, they were all a thing of beauty and just oozed cool. And the king of them all, the coolest, the baddest, and the most beautiful was without a doubt, the Jaguar XKE.

You can say what you want about Corvette, Trans Am, Dodge Charger, Lotus, etc., but nothing produced by any other car maker, on any continent, before or since, can compare to it. It had looks, power, and more style than you could shake a stick at. Hell, it looked like it was doing 120mph sitting in a parking lot. I've never owned one, my passion ran to MG TDs, but I still lust for one even to this day. And back in the spring of 1975 there were two of our illustrious classmates in D4 who had the good taste, and financial wherewithal, to make the XKE their first car; Mike Genetti and Jean-Luc Nash.

Genetti had a gorgeous (correct me if I'm wrong Mike) 1975 Silver XKE with a V-12 engine and JL purchased a used 1969 XKE, which was beautiful pale yellow. I never rode in Mike's but I did have a chance to ride with JL. He visited me one weekend at the garage where I was busy rebuilding my '51 MG with the help of a captain assigned to the Military Science Department at the Academy by the name of Hal Fuller.

Jean-Luc had Fuller do some minor work on his Jag and then he gave me a ride back to the Academy in time for Sunday supper formation. The car ran nicely and I remember very clearly the sensation of being pushed back into the seat as Jean-Luc accelerated down the road from a dead stop. I also still remember thinking to myself, "easy man, you don't need to run it to the red line every time before you shift." Needless to say, Jean-Luc really liked to accelerate quickly and drive fast.

Now Spring Break in April 1975 was a special time for all of us, mostly because it meant a week's leave, warmer climate, female companionship, and cruising in our new cars. Unfortunately for me, the MG was still being assembled so as the rest of you all headed South, I made my way to the garage in Vails Gate to what I hoped would be the final days of work before I was finished with the rebuild. I can't begin to tell you how that went over with Jen, my fiancé, who still reminds me about it to this day.

I remember clearly that first afternoon working on my car and the phone call that came into the shop. Fuller answered it, listened quietly, said some things and then hung up. Apparently one of my classmates from my company had broken down on the highway and was having his car towed to the shop.

Later that day, a tow truck pulled into the lot with the beautiful yellow Jag in tow and Jean-Luc, looking rather sheepish, riding shotgun. After it was unhooked, we pushed it into one of the bays to have a look. Now XKEs had a unique way of accessing the engine compartment; you unlatched the front body near the windshield and the whole thing swung up on a set of hinges near the front end, it's really cool. The frame is even better, it's a tubular arrangement that looks like something out of a Formula I race car. What we saw was even more impressive, the engine block had a half dollar size hole in the side. That was cool too since I'd never seen that before.

Apparently, Jean-Luc had thrown a rod and it blew its way out the side of the engine. Remember my comment about running it to the red line between shifts... it caught up with him. Now most of us would have been in a state of panic at the sight of that engine or at least near total depression, and Jean-Luc probably was. Fortunately for him, he could not have brought it to a more capable or resourceful mechanic, Hal Fuller. In no time Fuller was on the line, located a new engine from a salvage yard and had it delivered the next day.

So for the next few days Jean-Luc kept me company at the repair shop as he and Fuller worked to pull the old engine and install the new one. If I recall correctly, it only took them about two days to finish the job and the car was running again and Jean-Luc was on his way. Fuller didn't even charge him for the labor, only the engine and parts.

And that is how I got to spend Spring Break, Firstie Year, with Jean-Luc in an auto repair shop in Vails Gate. Eventually, I finished the MG but that is another story for another time. I don't know what happened to that Jag or how long he kept it.

Most of us who owned a British sports car came to the realization that they are more of a hobby and less of a reliable means of transportation, so we sold them and lived to regret it years later. Jean-Luc probably did too.

But I would imagine that he is now cruising in the land of perfectly maintained highways, neatly banked curves, 30 cent gas, looking down on us from the driver's seat of an XKE... and running it to the red line, every time."

Jean-Luc with his famous yellow 1969 Jaguar XKE

Keith Huber, Lieutenant General, US Army (retired)

General Huber took the time to call me and talk about JL. He and JL graduated from West Point at the same time but did not hang around each other as cadets. Jean-Luc was in D4 and Keith was in G4 at West Point.

Keith also remembers the 1969 yellow Jaguar that JL owned. It was infamous on campus apparently. The Jaguar had to be parked at an incline, the starter didn't work, and JL had to roll the car down a hill to get it started each and every time.

Jean-Luc was memorable to Keith because of his physical size, very tall and athletic. He rarely got angry, always had a sense of calmness about him, and was very resilient in any situation. I can vouch for that.

They both went through the Special Forces training together in January 1978 and obtained their Green Berets. Both went immediately to Scuba School in Florida, which is a Combat Divers School and is noted to be very difficult to pass. It was abnormal to do something like that so soon.

Keith remembers they were up at 4:30 am to make sure the '69 yellow Jaguar started and both would swim as a warm up before class began. The Combat Divers School lasted for a month. There were 38 attendees at the beginning, with a chosen class leader; yet only 11 graduated the combat diver's school. That is less than 30% completion.

The training consisted of exercise with weights in the pool. They basically drown you with the weights, then revive you. The cycle was repeated multiple times each day per student.

The original class leader quit; he was a Captain from the Army and was older than Keith and JL. The class leaders were chosen alphabetically so Keith became the class leader.

The last test was the "harassment swim" and it was down to the final 11 participants, those that didn't drop out yet. The test requires 2 participants; and if you do the math, someone would have to go twice since 11 is not an even number.

Jean-Luc already passed the final test and Keith was the last person, but didn't have a partner. So Jean-Luc volunteered. The drill was for 10 minutes and both participants have to stay underwater, at the bottom of the pool, for the entire 10 minutes.

A "double hose" is used; it is large in diameter and flexible, not thin or high pressure. You have to forcibly breathe through it. You and your partner have to share breaths through this double-house, which is called buddy breathing. To stay under, you make a knot at the bottom of the pool, wrapping your legs around each other, intertwined and sharing that hose.

Remember that Jean-Luc already did this earlier that day. He hadn't fully recovered from his first drill, so he got nauseous and threw up in the hose. Keith had to suck in JL's vomit in order to breathe. Oh. My. God. The instructors were amazed that neither of them broke the surface. Keith credits JL for helping him pass the Combat Divers School and it was only because JL volunteered.

After the Combat Divers School, Keith was sent to Panama and got a Scuba team. JL was assigned to Germany and met Stan Moore.

Stan Moore, Lieutenant Colonel, US Army (retired)

It was May of 1979 when Stan met Jean-Luc. Stan describes himself as a "fairly old" Captain and was the incoming new Detachment Commander, and Jean-Luc was the Detachment Executive Officer.

Stan had been in Special Forces before, in 5th Special Forces Group. The team was Operational Detachment 11, the Underwater Operations team, usually called the Scuba team. Jean-Luc had already been on the team for about a year. The team had about 9 men, including Jean-Luc and Stan.

They were stationed at Flint Kaserne, Bad Tolz, Germany. It was right on the edge of the Alps and a truly beautiful place. The Scuba team "owned" an Olympic length swimming pool that had been built for the Officer Training School of the Waffen SS before WWII.

JL and Stan got along well. They were both graduates of West Point, but neither of them were a typical West Point graduate. Neither cared much about promotions or doing things by the book. They both felt that rules were meant to be bent or broken. This was a good partnership for adventure and occasional disaster!

Stan's words: *I should describe JL at this time. Even in a Special Forces unit of unusual people, he was remarkably unusual. As anyone knows who ever met him, he was not one in a thousand or one in a million. He was totally unique; one of a kind. He was taller than average and much stronger than average. And he worked out with weights in a time when almost none of us did physical workouts other than morning physical training.*

His most unusual feature, however, was his attitude. **Jean-Luc was eternally optimistic**. *He was also completely pro-active. If anyone mentioned a new project or adventure, he'd say, "Let's go do it!"*

After discussion with Jean-Luc and the Team Sergeant, Master Sergeant RL Johnson, they decided to spend the warmer months of the summer training hard for their actual mission. They began making long trips, often for a week or so, to German lakes and doing extensive dive training.

RL Johnson developed a relationship with the German Wasserwacht (Coast Guard) and a German Army diving unit. They also did a lot of surface swimming, overland patrolling, shooting, and parachuting (mostly into water).

Here are a few stories that Stan shared:

Adventure of the corpse. One of the first actual missions they did together was a body recovery. An elderly German had disappeared while swimming in a lake and the Germans believed he was at the bottom. The German Coast Guard had a number of divers searching the small lake, were having no luck, and requested that the Scuba team assist.

At the end of a long summer day of diving and searching, the German Coast Guard stated that they would not return in the morning. The family of the deceased begged their Scuba team to return the next day, so they did. JL came up with an excellent method of doing a more organized search.

The old gentleman was found in the mud at the bottom of the little lake, glasses still on his nose. Many accolades were received for their success, both from the Germans and their chain of command. (That was a good thing. They would need those "attaboys" to cancel some later misadventures.)

Adventure on the Isar. For some reason, Stan owned a small inflatable canoe. It was not very stable. One very sunny weekend, JL and Stan decided to take a trip down the Isar, the local river, on that canoe. "The fact that young German ladies liked to sunbathe on the river banks wearing only their 'birth outfits' did not deter them from the mission." Jean-Luc and Stan were young and brave.

After about a mile, one of them shifted position in the little canoe and it flipped. Stan clearly remembers the water being extremely cold (it flowed from the Alps). They literally had just said, "Well, at least no one saw the 2 officers from the Scuba team flip a boat!" They looked up and saw a non-Special Forces warrant officer from the barracks fishing on the bank and laughing at them. Needless to say, JL and Stan ate a lot of crow on Monday. Humiliation is good for the soul.

Adventure of the angry helicopter. Late in the summer, Stan requested a large helicopter called a Chinook to support the team in its training. They did some parachuting from it into Lake Chiemsee. They then planned to surface swim on the lake and have the helicopter pick them up from the surface of the water. To demonstrate their great skills, Stan invited the Company Commander, Major Tony Salandro, to join them on the surface swim and pickup.

The original plan was that the Chinook helicopter would hover at the surface of the water with its large rear door open.

They'd all swim and crawl onto the floor of the helicopter through that rear ramp door. But...the pilot convinced Stan that they should go through the smaller door at the right front of the aircraft. So, they are in the middle of the lake. Their rucksacks are mission-packed and snapped onto a long climbing rope that connected them in a vague column of twos.

The monstrous Chinook hovers on the surface just in front of them. The wind is horrific from the 2 giant rotor blades. The lead swimmer is strong, makes it to the steps and up into the helicopter. He ties the rope to the steps. The other 9 of them struggle to swim forward because the helicopter is moving forward in the water.

Stan had a bad feeling and suddenly understood why: the helicopter is not only moving forward...it is sinking into the lake. Water had entered it from the rear ramp door. Not good. Major Salandro was caught under a fixture on the side of the helicopter and pulled underwater.

Suddenly, the engine noise became even louder. The pilot had become aware of his situation and applied maximum power and pitch to pull the helicopter upward. The big old helicopter groaned and slowly moved upward, water gushing out the sides and back.

The Special Forces soldiers were desperately trying to get away from it in the water, Stan and JL included. The aircraft suddenly became much lighter and zoomed upward. One of the team held on a little too long and fell about 20 feet into the water. Stan was certain one or more of the guys were dead. They weren't, but were all shaken up.

After they knew that all were OK, it was good for many laughs in the years ahead.

Adventure of the French prisoner. The French Army sent their group a message, inviting them to send an officer to visit one of their parachute units (RPIM, the French Special Forces) and participate in training for several weeks. Because JL spoke French and was in excellent physical condition, he was the obvious choice.

As Stan recalls, Jean-Luc left on a train on Sunday morning. On that same Sunday afternoon, Stan received a phone call, "Hey sir, I have a little problem…I'm in jail." The French border guard checked his passport, saw that he was born in France, and then arrested Jean-Luc for being a draft dodger!

JL was able to contact the U.S. Embassy fairly quickly and was released in the morning after their intervention. Stan believes the French decided to give him credit for his U.S. Army service time.

JL, in the center, with oxygen tanks on his back.

JL, on the right, on the German Alps from the late 70's

Dan Alexander, Colonel, US Army (retired)

"As the funeral started, the church choir mournfully sang Psalm 23, *The Lord Is My Shepard*. Tears welled up in my eyes and ran down my face. I made no effort to hide my sorrow at losing a friend who had been there for me in my hour of need. *The Lord is My Shepard* truly reflected Jean-Luc Marcel Nash's persona and spiritual beliefs."

As family, friends and D4 classmates sat stunned by the suddenness and improbability of what had just happened, God revealed to Dan the topic of his talk for Jean-Luc's wake later that night—Psalm 23 and the soulfulness of our departed Brother. Dan had memorized Psalm 23 in 1984, the first spiritual memorization he had done since plebe year at West Point.

Since then, whenever his physical and mental abilities reach a tipping point with challenges and tribulations, whenever his heart and soul roil in tumult, he turns to Psalm 23. And so it has been for him through war, divorce and Dan's own near-death experience and long recovery.

"In March 1991 in Iraq, casualties in US 3rd Armored Division and VII Corps, in general, were mounting even though the 1st Gulf War was technically over. Losing friends after the shooting stopped was not a part of war we had expected. Thousands of Shiites were being butchered in front of us by a despot we had supposedly beaten into submission."

"We were handcuffed by the UN and unable to do anything about it. With this backdrop, Jean-Luc reentered to my life at a critical moment. Every day during this deployment, whenever I woke up or went to sleep, I meditated on Psalm 23. While driving south on the Basra-Kuwait City Highway (Highway 8), through the Mutla Pass, running the "Highway of Death" I could not help but think "Yeah though I walk through the valley of the shadow of death I fear no evil thy Rod and Staff they comfort me." Upon arriving at a deposed Kuwaiti Prince's Palace recently liberated from the Iraqi III Corps, I immediately bumped into of all people, "Ranger" Nash."

Dan had not seen Jean-Luc since Graduation Day, June 4, 1975. There were a hundred grads at the 1991 West Point Founder's Day celebration in Kuwait City, but Dan only remembers one person, Jean-Luc. No one was really celebrating; they were all just thankful to still be alive and enjoying the brotherhood, talks and briefings as humble victors.

Jean-Luc and Dan sat down on the floor next to each other and began to talk and share everything about the last three months, like they had been talking as best friends continuously for a lifetime. Jean-Luc was a very deep and spiritual soul, when the situation called for it. Yes, he was physically powerful and mentally strong, but what Dan remembers from that night was his thoughtful listening and sharing at a deep, soulful level.

Dan remembers saying to himself afterward that he had never really known the real Jean-Luc until then. To him, Jean-Luc was God's instrument that night; he led Dan to quiet pastures and beside still waters; he restored Dan's soul.

"He set a table before me in the presence of our enemies … our cups runneth over… Best Founder's Day I have ever attended. I'll never forget the Brotherhood we shared that night!"

"Thank you for being there for me, Jean-Luc. I look forward to our prayerful talks each night until we meet again, Brother."

Dan received a heart transplant in the summer of 2016, about 5 months after Jean-Luc's funeral. Dan never mentioned to us that he was on a transplant list; we learned about it after the fact.

He received the heart of Bryan Clausen, a race car driver that lost his life after a crash at Belleville 2016, a short dirt track race. Bryan was 27 at the time of his death and was an organ donor who ended up saving multiple lives such as Dan's.

THE CHALLENGE

One of the first things my mother told me after Jean-Luc's death was that she took him for granted. She expected him to always be there for her. She expected to die first. We all took him for granted actually. Jean-Luc became the backbone of our extended family. He was the glue that kept it all together.

The Family Life

Life in general is difficult and can be messy if you think about it. Family dynamics can be undeniably complicated. Throw in being part of a military family - as a child or spouse of a soldier - this adds less stability to your life. You don't always feel like you "fit in" because you move around a lot or you don't ever see your father because they are deployed.

The family environment no doubt has the biggest influence on you and can affect your expectations and decisions. My perspectives in life were influenced by being part of a military family. There was always a lot of uncertainty and unexpected situations. This lifestyle can be difficult on every family member, particularly the spouse.

As a child of a soldier, you don't have to personally risk your life yet you still feel the effects. How do you deal with that? This can help you be better prepared for what life throws at you. I learned to focus on the positive aspects and to expect the good through my stepfather.

The positive perspective of a family situation like mine is you can learn to embrace each of those changes as another adventure. Jean-Luc emphasized that.

A common viewpoint is that those who choose to serve in the military are innately drawn to helping others in some shape or form. It's not about *them*. There's a humbleness and JL showcased that humility.

After my biological father died at the Atlanta VA hospital, JL went out of his way to tell me that he was sorry about my father's passing. This was not out of character for JL, he had an instinctive diplomacy, he treated everyone with respect and knew the right thing to say. There was an unspoken connection my brother and I had with JL; he didn't spend much time with his biological father either.

JL is an example of overcoming issues and obstacles and not relying on excuses. This was his mindset: if you have trouble making logical decisions, try learning about tough-mindedness and how to develop more psychological resistance.

We first met his parents and two sisters, Colleen and Nicole, at Jean-Luc's wedding to our mother. I was one of the bridesmaids and my younger sister was the flower girl. They had a December wedding and I do remember the dress being hot-as-hell to wear because the material was a heavy velvet, burgundy in color.

What's impressive is that my mother made all the bridesmaids dresses and the flower girl dress, a total of 6 dresses! Sewing is a skill I didn't inherit from her by the way.

Jean-Luc had his father's demeanor. His name was Gerald and he had a warm personality and was pleasant. (I guess it's okay to refer to him as my grandfather). Gerald was a Warrant Officer and a helicopter pilot for the Army; his last military assignment was in Alaska and that's where he retired from the military. Alaska is where JL considered his home state.

Gerald had an RV and drove cross country multiple times. Gerald replaced it with a brand-new RV at the time of his second retirement and decided to settle in Arizona. One of his last cross-country stops included Georgia to see my family. But the retirement and enjoying the new RV didn't last long. Gerald died 6 months after retirement from Civil Service (his 1st retirement was from the Army).

Gerald was born in 1936 and passed away in Arizona July 11, 1999 after brain tumor surgery. He had lung cancer that had metastasized to his brain. The hospital in Arizona kept Gerald on a ventilator so that Jean-Luc could return from the Democratic Congo to say goodbye in person. Then they unplugged him. That was heart-breaking.

My mom was in Alexandria, VA at the time as a Research Psychologist for the U.S. Army out of Walter Reed Hospital. Her office was connected to the Pentagon. One of her brothers and his family literally just arrived from France, and my mom couldn't attend the funeral of her father-in-law. That caused a bit of tension with my mom and JL.

The death of his father was the first time we saw Jean-Luc outwardly sad and upset. Gerald was of American Indian descent and wanted to be cremated.

Jean-Luc spread his father's ashes over Arizona from a helicopter. The wind was strong and blew his father's ashes right back into JL's face and he was totally covered in his father's ashes. JL said "Dad was probably laughing at me in heaven."

JL's mother, Andree Nash, was French like my mother. She met Gerald while he was stationed in France, married Gerald when JL was 6 years old and they moved to the US shortly afterward. This is a typical story – an American soldier meets a girl overseas.

Andree lived alone in Arizona for a while after Gerald passed away, but that was hard on her with no family around. JL did take a cross country trip one Summer with the three oldest grandsons (Brent, Eric, and Hudson) to visit her in Arizona. Andree passed away at the age of 79 while having heart surgery in January 2012. We were all able to attend her funeral because she lived in Alabama near one of her daughters.

JL and his mom, Andree, enjoying a cruise beach stop

Meeting the Family (requires Patience)

My mother and Jean-Luc met in an interesting way, something I didn't learn until I was an adult. After being assigned to Fort Benning, JL received a notice from the French government for being a draft dodger (remember Stan Moore's story...). The document was in French and even though his own mother was French, he needed help with translating it.

The situation was complicated. He was born in France so that makes him a natural-born citizen of France. He had two choices. Meet with the French Liaison Officer in Fort Benning or with my mother who was fluent in French and has dual citizenship. Jean-Luc told my mom he decided to start with her because she was prettier.

According to Jean-Luc, while in Germany, he received orders to join Parachute Training with the French Army. It was a Saturday evening when he crossed the border and arrived at a checkpoint. The gendarme (armed police officer in France) asked for JL's passport, and immediately noticed that he was born in Nancy, France. Like a good detective, the guard went to his rolodex and checked for the list of draft dodgers. In France, all males must serve two years in the Army during that timeframe.

The guard informed Jean-Luc that he was being arrested for draft dodging. Jean-Luc called the US Embassy and his company commander...he had to spend the night in jail and was freed the next day by some French Army Officers.

Jean-Luc became the first West Point graduate thrown in jail for being a draft dodger. A Captain at that. He was never able to live down that infamous reputation.

I look back at photos of my mother when she was younger, the timeframe that Jean-Luc met her, and she was definitely pretty, actually she was gorgeous. Many of my friends have told me that.

My mom has a lot of "spunk" and JL saw this as a challenge. They were quite opposite in personality.

From the moment my mother introduced JL to her children – after my parents' divorce - I was indifferent toward Jean-Luc for the first two years. As a 16-year-old you think you know everything and I felt he was intruding into my blissful existence. Yet JL was calm in that first encounter with me. My brother was a college student and came across as more mature than me; well, because he was.

The divorce happened right before my junior year of high school and didn't help my attitude. After the divorce, there was tension at home with my adopted father. I was expected to take care of the house (cook, clean, do laundry), take care of my little sister, get a part-time job, continue to participate in sports, and continue making good grades. That was a lot of pressure.

There was an athletic scholarship opportunity for me at Georgia Tech. My adopted father described how dangerous the Tech location was (it was in Atlanta!) and I was a girl. *What did being a girl have to do with it?* He was concerned I would be sexually assaulted on campus. That fed the fear.

This was also when the Title IX amendment was fairly new; it prohibits discrimination on the basis of your sex through any federally funded education program or activity. I was afraid to make a decision and pretended everything was okay.

My mom and JL offered me to live with them; so I decided to move to North Carolina after high school graduation in 1983. I really didn't have a place to live after graduating from high school or money to pay for college. My grades were very good, but again, zero funds. Moving in with them provided stability and JL realized that was needed.

Jean-Luc bought my first car, a white 1976 Datsun B-210. It was a stick shift as well, so he had to teach me how to drive it too. That probably tested his patience but I remember he stayed calm and I learned quickly. He didn't yell once. He also told me that knowing how to drive a stick shift will help me drive anything. This was very helpful information.

The transmission went out on the Datsun after about 30 days so he had it towed to the carpool on base at Fort Bragg and planned to repair it himself. He made me come with him to the carpool and watch. It was awkward because we were still getting to know each other. Mobile phones weren't invented yet so I didn't have an "escape" like teens do today.

To this day, I'm not sure if my lack of shifting gear experience led to the transmission failure. He didn't give me too much crap about it.

We did have something in common though. Running. Being outside for a run is something JL and I like to do.

The first thing I ever did with JL was run outside on the road near Augusta, GA. It was the middle of summer, hot and humid. I was on the cross-country team, running was something I was into, and was supposed to practice anyway over the summer.

This was when my mom worked at Fort Gordon, before they were married. JL would visit on weekends when his schedule allowed. My sister and I stayed with our mom for a while over the summer before my senior year of high school.

And the last thing I ever did with JL was run outside together on Christmas Day. This was almost 34 years apart. He told me on that day he enjoyed staying at our house because of the trail access to the woods. JL was smiling as he said this and I could see that sparkle in his eyes.

Exercising made him happy and JL liked to work out every day. He did it like clockwork and loved to reference military time regardless of the situation.

No one had used the "basement gym" since he passed away in that room working out, doing his daily regimen. I decided to "open up the gym" again and encourage others to use the equipment when visiting my mom. That's what he would want anyway.

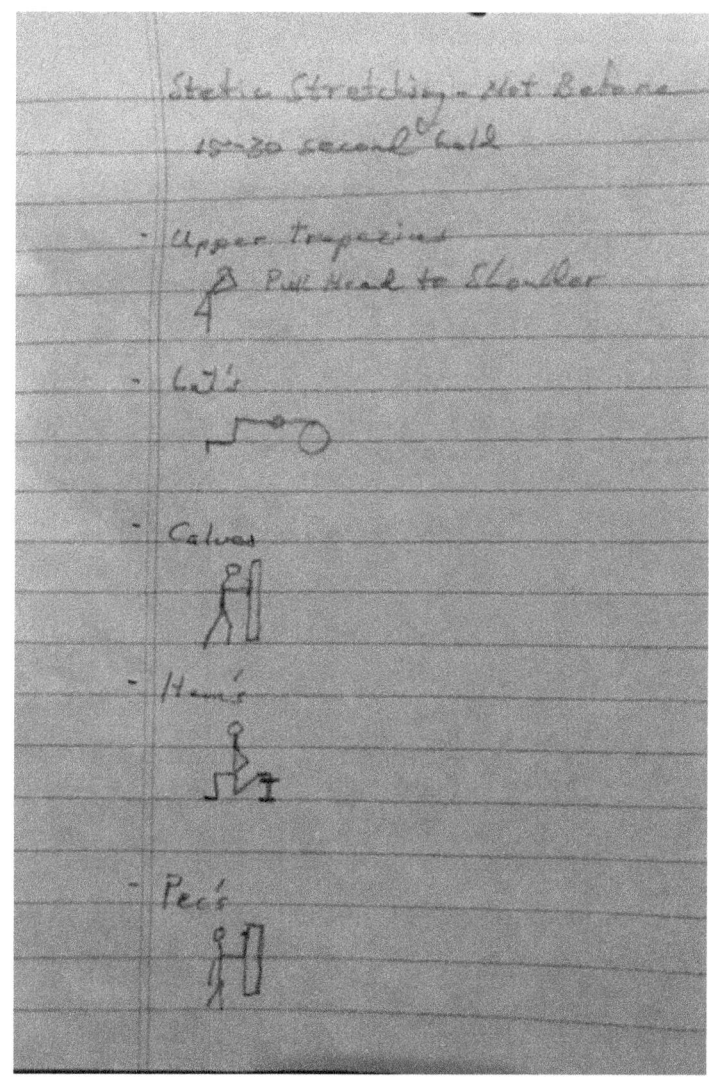

I found this workout schedule laying on JL's treadmill dashboard.

The Meet-up

My mom provided more specifics about their first meeting. JL was attending the Infantry Advanced Course in 1981 and she was an intern at the Research and Development for The Infantry School in Fort Benning, Georgia. She remembers that a tall Captain stood in front of her desk, requesting assistance with some French translation. My mom is not sure who referred JL to her, but graciously accepted to assist him.

The official document he handed over looked like a military draft paper, informing him that in a case of conflict, he would be drafted as an E-1 in the French Army. He was instructed to provide an acknowledgement and response to the missive. She showed him how to reply to the French document.

The translation should have taken only 10 minutes at the most. However, he was able to converse and pull all kinds of information out of my mom for four hours. He missed four hours of instruction and she wasted four hours of work according to her.

She was fascinated by that Captain for some reason. He was not fazed by the awkward situation, took everything in stride, knew my mom's life story, and didn't divulge anything about himself ... such as was he married, engaged, had a girlfriend?

Frustrated and angry at herself for sharing too much info at their initial meeting, she searched for his phone number through the rosters and found out he was single. A few days later, she nonchalantly called and asked him if he heard from the French Army. He replied "yes" and after a few minutes of conversation, he asked her out for a date. Unknown to her, he was dating two other ladies at that time.

No wonder he was so nonchalant.

Everything was going smoothly, they had a few dates before she was transferred to Fort Gordon, Georgia, which was part of her internship and contract. Jean-Luc decided to take her for a weekend date to Atlanta before the transfer to Fort Gordon.

They went to the Six Flags Over Georgia Park, walked for over 12 hours and had a blast. The next morning at breakfast, Jean-Luc announced to her with a strange statement: "Michele, I want you to know that I will never get married; so don't expect me to marry you, it will never happen."

She was baffled, angry, and replied: "You are the most conceited, arrogant man I ever met. Who wants to marry you? And I do not want to get married, who needs it."

"Why do you date me or any man?" was his reply.

"Well, someone has to pay for my meals, movies, theater tickets, etc."

"I want to inform you that I have a few girlfriends."

"Same here, I have a few boyfriends myself."

"Fine, we are on the same sheet of music as it appears."

One week after that trip to Six Flags, Jean-Luc called and asked for another date. She told him that she had to check her "black book" where she kept track of all the appointments. My mom then told him that she had dates booked for the next two weekends (not true).

He reluctantly accepted to reserve a date for the third weekend. The following week the same thing happened. He requested a date, hoping someone canceled out or got very sick.

After two months of this treatment, he blew up on a phone call - "Okay, okay, you won, I don't want you to date anyone else but me. It tears me up to know that another man kisses or touches you. As for me, I will have only one girl friend – You!"

For a man who didn't want to get married, he pursued her relentlessly.

The Department of Defense contract with my mom was for twelve months. She couldn't resign before that time or she would have to reimburse all the moving expenses and TDY payments.

Two weeks after her contract at Fort Gordon ended, Jean-Luc rented a moving truck and moved all her belongings to Fayetteville, NC and they got married shortly after. This was a lot of change happening in a short amount of time.

After their marriage and being comfortably "installed" as a spouse of a military officer, Jean-Luc encouraged my mom to be "reinstalled" as a government employee. He also supported that she "be herself" because she had a lot to offer.

Two months after their wedding, an employment opportunity came up. My mom was asked to go in for an interview as an Education Counselor at the Army Education Center. Upon arriving, she was informed there were seven total candidates, and two of them held a doctorate degree.

She was the last candidate to be interviewed by a panel of five judges. The panel leader informed her that the responses will be recorded. She noticed a legal yellow pad with several pages with information on the previous candidates. The interview was very boring and the responses were yes or no to the questions that were asked.

At the end of the interview, she saw that only two lines were filled out on her interview page: her name and her degrees versus the other candidates ... who could jump off from a speeding train and stop bullets with only one hand. She knew she was in trouble.

The leader asked if she could tell the panel why they should hire her. She didn't know at that moment if she could stop herself from crying and be able to bluff her way out.

Thankfully, she gained control and told them, "Last night I was watching TV and I saw President Reagan making a plea to all the employers to hire an unemployed person and he would be grateful for any hiring. Therefore, make President Reagan happy, hire me, and he will be very grateful to all of you, and so would I." The meeting ended with laughter.

When she arrived at home, Jean-Luc asked how the interview went. She replied "...poorly." Lo and behold the next day, the Civilian Personnel called and told her that she was chosen for the position.

This confirms where my sister and I get our sassiness from.

My high school graduation was less than four months after my mom was hired for this position. JL and my mom drove to Georgia (over 7 hours) to attend. It was awkward to have my my mom and "my fathers" attend the graduation, and I didn't appreciate the effort at the time. It was about 'me.' Again, this situation didn't seem to faze JL.

I moved to North Carolina shortly after the graduation and settled into their new house. That's when JL bought me the car. My mom helped me enroll at Campbell University and they paid for the tuition. My younger sister, Michele, stayed with us over the summer and went back home to Georgia once school started. She was 10 years old at the time.

Michele and I hung out at the Officer's Club pool as much as possible over that summer and I charged our lunches to JL's account. Our tans were great. I delayed interacting with others because deep down I was scared of the future – mine and my little sister's.

This is how I remember Jean-Luc - the timeframe when he met and then married our mom. My first impression was "this is a badass."

An Unexpected Departure

My first semester of college started in September and was going smoothly. I didn't see JL much because of my class schedule and I had a part-time job to pay for gas for the Datsun B-210 and other minor expenses. JL included me on their car insurance policy and was paying for that. Another thing I took for granted at the time.

One evening in October 1983, the wife of the Brigade S-3 commander called and told my mother that all the spouses from the Second Brigade, 82d Airborne Division would meet at an informal gathering. The commander's wife volunteered to pick her up.

My mom was surprised to find out that their meeting was at a nightclub! It was a ladies' night special and they were to be treated to a male strip tease. She was very uncomfortable and felt out of place. All the wives there cheered, applauded and she wanted to hide underneath the chair. That was her first male strip tease and her last, and didn't like it at all.

After that long evening, the commander's wife drove her back home. There was a note waiting on her bed pillow:

"Darling, sorry I missed you to say good bye. All Second Brigade headquarters soldiers are being deployed in a hurry, unable to tell where. Remember that I love you forever. J.L."

It dawned on her at that moment…the Brigade tried to keep all the wives occupied because they had to deploy the troops in hurry. She went to bed very sad that night and feeling guilty that she was at a male strip club while her husband was risking his life doing his job.

After a few weeks, the troops all returned home. Jean-Luc didn't say too much about what happened. Turns out he was in Grenada.

One morning a few weeks after returning home, JL called my mom's office and asked her to participate in a Brigade ceremony. As a good military wife she agreed. It was a surprise to see him standing with two other soldiers in front of a Brigade formation. She was even more surprised when the Brigade read the citation that Jean-Luc was being recognized for his courage and valor during a conflict in Grenada.

He saved the lives of two soldiers during an attack; his quick decision and disregard of the danger to himself. He never said a word about it to me or my mom. Later she asked him "why" and he replied "that was part of his job and there was nothing to tell." She was so proud of him…for his courage, quick decision making and modesty.

JL then told her, "Leave this world a better place than you entered." This became his motto to the family and he repeated it over the years, especially his grandkids.

Operation Urgent Fury

There's an important piece of history we don't hear much about or have forgotten. It's the Grenada invasion of 1983, also known as Operation Urgent Fury.

President Reagan stepped in and built a large army to fight in Grenada to essentially do the right thing - protect Americans and go against the corruption of a country that was being invaded and seized by American enemies.

Jean-Luc received the Bronze Star with a "V" for Valor for the lives he saved during Operation Urgent Fury. This is very prestigious and awarded for heroism in combat. The bronze star is awarded at 3 levels and "V" is the highest level, meaning he put his life at risk to save others.

He never shared this story much less bragged about it. My mom didn't know about it until she was invited to the ceremony at Fort Bragg and saw him actually receive the medal. Jean-Luc told her that he was just doing his job and is what he signed up for.

Side note, my husband was part of the Grenada operation too and I didn't know him at the time. He was a paratrooper in the 82nd Airborne and arrived less than a week after the invasion, and stayed for 2 weeks to help patrol the island.

Here's some background to better understand by answering the who, what, when, where, and why the U.S. went to Grenada in the first place.

Grenada Background

Grenada is a former British colony that is located 400 miles south of Puerto Rico. It is an island country and sovereign state, comprised of the island of Grenada itself as well as six smaller islands. Turmoil was created after a group of determined Marxists seized power in 1979. Even more chaos erupted when Cuba's Fidel Castro became involved.

The Soviet Union then aided Cuba in building a large airport (with a 9,000 foot runway) that quickly posed as a threat to the US national security. It was a big risk because of the close proximity of Grenada to the United States.

President Ronald Reagan began to form a military buildup that eventually was sent to Grenada to put a stop to this. In addition, there were 600 U.S. students studying in Grenada's capital, which raised the fear of hostages being taken like Iran had done in 1980. The U.S. operations initial attacks involved approximately 800 Marines, 650 Rangers, and 60 Special Operations fighters.

On Grenada's side, there were approximately 600 soldiers from Grenada's regular army, and their militia would add another 2,500-2,800 bodies. Most of them ignored the call to mobilize and chose not to respond. The Cuban influence on the island was over 700 people, which was made up of 53 military advisors and 636 construction workers (many having military experience).

The concern about Grenada and its impact on the U.S. began in 1979, however, it took a few years for the Operation itself to start.

It all began in late October 1982, when stormy weather stopped two attempts made by the Navy SEALS and Air Force combat controllers to scout the island.

Other than the weather, a major drawback of the missions was the lack of safe landing zones. The U.S. Marines who were involved had already heard that things weren't off to a good start, and many got very little sleep that night with a small meal and preparing for what would be the first exposure to combat for most of them. Fortunately, when light came and they were able to land with no opposition, the Marines fired back after hearing gunfire. After hearing the return fire, the militia ran away and there were no casualties on either side.

The citizens of Grenada were smiling and even helped the U.S. soldiers by pointing out militia members, and weapon sites and vehicles used to steal captured US weapons. Things weren't going very well for the Rangers located in the south part of the island. Jean-Luc's group was part of this. They suffered light casualties trying to clear obstacles to the runway. When they arrived at the medical school to protect the 600 American students believed to be there, they found that most of them were at other locations.

The Special Operations missions around St. George's Island also encountered trouble. A SEAL team member was driven away from a radio-transmission received, and after intense fire, an Army helicopter was knocked down, killing or injuring almost all who were on board. Twenty-two SEALs were pinned down by counterattacks and Rangers suffered more casualties in an ambush. The U.S. called for more battalions after believing they were facing a stronger enemy than anticipated and six more battalions of paratroopers came three days later.

The Cobras also faced trouble and were exposed to deadly fire that the Delta Force had been previously exposed to. After being ordered to take the Grenadian headquarters at Fort Frederick, the Marines showed up to find it abandoned. Two Battalions of paratroopers attacked and captured the Cuban positions northeast of the airport terminal. Cuban resistance was finally over but the Americans were unaware at the time being.

A Ranger mission to find a large group of the students who weren't at the main campus was met with fire, but when the Rangers organized and made it to the school, the opposition vanished. The students were taken to safety and the US moved on the other areas to expand their control. Marines were being sent on multiple missions to the northern and southern sectors. The Marines eventually occupied about two-thirds of the island's coastline.

After a week of endless missions and small successes met with light but nonetheless heartbreaking tragedies, the Marines landed on Grenada's northern island on November 1 to be greeted by friendly citizens and 19 soldiers in civilian clothes, who then surrendered.

These are two great quotes found on the official Marine Corps website that shed light on the military and how they themselves may look back on Grenada, and how intense it was for them regardless of the victory:

"Although ultimately successful, the multi-service attack on Grenada, code-named Operation Urgent Fury, would be noted for poor intelligence, communications and interoperability and, in some instances, for timid leadership."

"But Urgent Fury would also demonstrate again the flexibility, versatility and the well-honed capabilities of a Navy-Marine Corps amphibious task force."

Source (official marine corps site with details of operation): https://www.mca-marines.org/leatherneck/operation-urgent-fury-grenada

Source (40 min documentary covering operation I watched parts of for visual/factual background): https://www.youtube.com/watch?v=LTJEI4yeVSY

Source (for basic geography/facts of Grenada and its location in terms of the US): http://www.worldatlas.com/webimage/countrys/namerica/caribb/gd.htm

Harry's Story

"People often ask what courage is, and to me, it's hope."
~Harry Shaw

I finally met Harry Shaw in person at Jean-Luc's funeral. He and Jean-Luc connected again after JL retired from the military and they became friends.

Harry Shaw gravitated toward an outdoor lifestyle and could not wait to get out of high school. You can join the National Guard when you're 17 years old; you just need your parents' permission. He got permission and completed the National Guard training between his junior and senior year.

After high school graduation, Harry immediately volunteered to join the Army and decided to go Airborne. This was December 1981, right around the time Ronald Reagan started the big military buildup. "It is an honor to be part of the Airborne and there was never a lack of confidence."

Harry was based in Fort Bragg, NC and distinctly remembers when they got THE "call-out." There were several call-outs before Grenada and nothing happened. A call-out has you prep and lay out your military gear and it all gets inspected. You can go back upstairs, you're good to go and can go back to what you were doing before.

Except the last call-out was different. The First Sergeant said "I hate to tell you but this one's for real. We need to go."

This all happened a day or two after the Marines had been bombed in Beirut. The expectation was that they were going to Lebanon at first; Harry and his fellow Airborne troops were certain of it. Except they were told Grenada was the destination. Most of them had never heard of the place and they had all this cold weather gear. That type of gear couldn't be used in Grenada, they were told to just leave it, and worry about putting the gear away when they returned.

As an E-4, Harry was part of the initial invasion of Grenada with the Airborne Division. The troops had rigged and de-rigged their parachutes a few times on the plane; and only thirty minutes prior to their arrival, it was decided they would air land. They ended up having to take their chutes off and that really pissed them off because they were expecting to parachute in. That was the wrong mood to send them into battle and defeat the enemy Harry jokingly recalled. Regardless, the mission was continued.

The second morning in Grenada was when Harry met Captain Jean-Luc Nash. Harry originally was in field artillery of the 82nd Airborne and had trained with the Fire Support team. Harry's Battalion Sergeant Major Damers told Harry they needed him to help over in the Second Brigade attack. He grabbed his gear and showed up to work with Jean-Luc.

Jean-Luc was a Captain in the Tactical Operations Center, the headquarters for the Second Brigade. They were stationed right at the north end of the runway and coordinating support fires for the invasion.

"On the third morning, there was a security escort meeting and CNN had reporters show up. The reporters wanted a pass to go wherever they wanted. That wasn't a good idea." Harry doesn't know how the reporters got on the island in the first place.

That same day in the early afternoon, the Second Brigade moved forward and targeted some barracks that could be taken over; this happened in a 4 hour timeframe on the third day. Prior to that, the troops were sitting out in the open for two and a half days. They were happy to have a roof at least. There were some old mattresses and old equipment that was just thrown out the window.

About another 4 hours later, the barracks came under enemy fire from 3 different locations. The barracks were up on a ridge and they could see it all. In return, several hundred rounds of artillery were fired and some airstrikes were happening. Two of the targets had been neutralized and at the same time they were using 87's and field artillery to coordinate with the Rangers.

There was a gun-run by the Air Force with 20-millimeter high explosives and there was a tragic mistake. The pilot hit the wrong building. The building was thought to be empty but there were three soldiers inside: Harry Shaw, Sean Lukatina, and Sergeant Joey Stewart.

Harry remembers looking out the window and up as the plane was leveling with the building. He said to Sean, who was sitting next to him, "Sean, I think they're coming here!" Harry turned, moved and got cut down by artillery.

Sean had substantial shrapnel injuries. Both of Harry's legs were shattered but he didn't realize it at the time how serious his situation was. He wondered how much blood he could lose and still be alive. There was never a more desperate time in his life.

There were fourteen wounded soldiers outside the building and Captain Jean-Luc Nash asked the question, "Is anybody in the barracks?" He was told "No, everybody's outside." Checking the barracks didn't seem important to others at the moment.

Then Jean-Luc asked another question "Shouldn't somebody check?" JL decided to go in to take a look. He came back out and asked Spec4 Tim Andruss to accompany him back in the building that was just hit with explosives.

These are Harry's words: "In that few minutes after being hit, Jean-Luc suddenly appeared over me."

Here's an excerpt of what Harry beautifully wrote on his blog as soon as he learned of Jean-Luc's death:

"I know a lot about the depths of desperation and despair and loss, but, nothing in my life has compared to the absolute sense of loss of this great, giant of a man. There is a hole in the world and there is a hole in the depths of my heart. Superlatives pale in comparison to the magnitude of greatness that was Jean-Luc Nash. I did not know him before we invaded Grenada on October 25th, 1983. There has not been a day that has passed since then, that I have not thought of him.

What transpired on that bloody battleground was more than lives (my own included) being saved. One cannot truly understand the depths of true brotherhood until one has shared the absolute intensities and desperations and depravations of warfare. Jean-Luc Nash did more than make it possible for me to have a chance at surviving that day. He gave me countless opportunities.

I will forever reach out to you and the memory of who you were, and seek to be worthy of the faith you had in my life."

Tim's Perspective

Harry connected me with Tim Andruss and Tim was kind enough to provide his perspective on Operation Urgent Fury. Tim is now a firefighter and EMT in the state of Washington. And I so appreciate him sharing his story. Harry, Jean-Luc and Tim stayed in touch after all those years.

Tim remembers the specific date. Grenada, October 25th, 1983. On a ridge whose name is forgotten. These are Tim's words:

"We occupied a simple wooden two room building on this prominence, after locating the Brigade TOC (Tactical Operations Center) here some hours earlier. I recall the structure had served as a barracks for the Grenadian Militia until the invasion commenced two days prior. Three or four radios were being monitored in the smaller room, leaving the larger portion open for cautious observation onto the valley beneath.

Radio traffic coordinated movement of a platoon from the Second Brigade making their way across the lowland before us. They were accompanied by a Navy FAC (Forward Air Coordinator). Our "unit" was made up of HHC, Second Brigade and various attachments. *(HHC is Headquarters and Headquarters Company – an army Battalion).*

At some point during the afternoon, we began receiving sniper fire from a ridgeline across the valley. Everyone was ordered out of the building but three or four soldiers who were left to monitor radio traffic. We assumed protective cover behind the structure and some cinder blocks piled to its side.

The unit in the valley worked to ascertain the precise location of the sniper. The Naval FAC called in an air strike by a

Sortie of three A7 Corsairs off an aircraft carrier, USS Independence. The A7's mistakenly swept in on our position and fired their 20mm cannons. In my recollection, only the first two aircraft fired.

The burst of gunfire was both deafening as well as physically palpable as the structure and surroundings splintered and shattered under the explosive impact. Several of the cinder blocks that provided cover for many of us also crumbled from the shrapnel. While bits of wood still rained down, the soldiers who were inside on the radios ran out, each with various shrapnel wounds.

I placed gauze pressure bandages on a couple soldiers with non-life-threatening wounds. After what was probably only 60 seconds, Captain Nash called my name, summoning me from the doorway into the "barracks end" of the structure.

My memory of it has always remained that he was deceptively calm at that moment and I can still picture him in the doorway. He had already entered the structure to survey the damage and found the first of two grievously wounded soldiers inside. This was Harry Shaw.

Harry had been attached to our HHC the day before as a liaison from the artillery unit. Harry was last seen peering out of the window on the valley side of the building, perhaps trying to locate the source of the incoming small arms fire.

I distinctly recall Master Sergeant Al Harris from S3 saying "those that want to look are those that want to die." MSG Harris had done a few tours in Vietnam and clearly had no fascination with the novelty of battle. He had been speaking directly to a few individuals who were tempted enough to peer out from the structure.

Anyway, back to Jean-Luc. He had summoned me to assist him in treating Harry who had clearly received 20mm gunshot and shrapnel wounds to his lower and upper legs and torso. The femur of each leg had been shattered. Harry's right lower leg was folded laterally around to position the toes of that boot pointing at, and resting beside his right hip.

Quite surprisingly, Harry was conscious and asking what had happened, not expressing pain, but confusion, clearly in shock and trying to sit up. He couldn't understand why he couldn't sit. I had to hold him to the ground to keep him from seeing his injuries. Jean-Luc was doing his best to straighten the legs so we could take some measures to stop the bleeding.

I grabbed the laces out of a pair of boxing gloves hanging from the rafters to use as tourniquets. Jean-Luc tied them around the portion of Harry's legs that were still connected to his torso while I continued to try and keep Harry conscious, repeatedly asking him questions.

While we crouched over Harry, the A7 aircraft made another diving pass low over our heads and I think we BOTH were expecting them to open fire again. A helpless moment! I do recall that as we worked on Harry, several soldiers entered the room and immediately left upon seeing the situation.

We used the front door of the building to serve as a stretcher. We wrapped a poncho over Harry and made our way out of the building and about 300 yards down a dirt road to an open field to wait for an incoming medivac helicopter. I don't know how long we waited but I don't think it was more than a minute, maybe two. When the helicopter touched down we carried Harry out and loaded him up and off they went to a hospital ship.

Captain Nash and I then went back to the building and into the other end of the structure where we had set up the TOC (Tactical Operations Center). There we found another individual with similar major injuries, Sean Lukatina. He was also attached to HHC from the same artillery unit as Harry. I do not recall his injuries as clearly as Harry's.

JL and I loaded Sean on top of a door...perhaps the same door used for Harry, and once again made our way to the landing zone for his extraction. I recall that as we loaded him onto the helicopter, the poncho blew off and swirled in the wind from the prop wash. I ran and dove on it before it could become entangled in the rotors. The second chopper disappeared overhead.

Sean had shrapnel injuries to his legs and spine, and he died about 9 months later of a persistent infection to his spine and was in a coma the majority of the time.

My general recollection of Captain Jean-Luc Nash was one of calm intensity. I don't believe that he had any combat exposure prior to Grenada, nor had I, but we had both been through Ranger School and I think that does prepare one well for functioning under duress.

During my roughly year and a half working in the Second Brigade S3 with him, I don't recall ever seeing Jean-Luc worked up when things were going sideways.

He impressed me as an honorable man who treated each soldier he encountered with the same respect, regardless of rank or background. I consider myself fortunate to have worked alongside your stepdad."

Defense Language Institute

My sister just finished 6th grade and moved in with JL and my mom the summer of 1984. Having an 11-year-old around was a different responsibility. JL took it in stride though.

I didn't help take care of her much in that timeframe because of college and working, and wanted to spend as much time with my boyfriend of course.

Then about a year later came JL's next military assignment at the Naval Postgraduate School and the Defense Language Institute. This is where he studied for his Masters in International Studies and one year at the language school.

Being accepted into the Defense Language Institute (DLI) is another example of Jean-Luc's intellect and drive. DLI is based in the Presidio of Monterey, CA and part of the Department of Defense.

The language JL learned was Arabic – a very difficult language to say the least - and he spent 8 hours daily in the classroom, studied at night and most of the weekend. My mother said learning Arabic was difficult for him, but he never complained or got discouraged. He kept on pushing through, every day, in typical Jean-Luc fashion.

Knowing the Arabic language allowed him to become a Defense Attaché later on. Officers in that role work around the world in U.S. Embassies within a Defense Attaché Office (DAO).

The DAO represents the Department of Defense to the host-nation government and military, assists and advises the U.S.

Ambassador on military matters, and coordinates other political-military actions within their area of accreditation.

There is one other person I knew that attended DLI besides Jean-Luc. My high school friend, Mike Ray, decided to join the Army after graduating from the University of Alabama. He did well on the ASVAB test and that opened the door for him to attend the DLI near Monterey. His language of choice was Russian. That was also right around the time the Cold War ended.

I reached out to Mike to ask him about his experience and get his perspective of DLI. All of the military branches are represented, not just the Army. You attend classes Monday thru Friday, for at least 7 hours each day in class learning your target language. There was also two to three hours of homework each night. Mike's training lasted a year.

Each student went back to their respective barracks to study at the end of the day. The soldiers from the different branches were kept separate, didn't really socialize. The students attended class in their military uniform that corresponds to their branch of service.

The students had to continue with physical training to meet the standards of their service. The service commanders ensured the service members continue what was necessary to also complete their military mission and to make sure they're combat ready. Mike commented that the Marines seemed to have it the hardest based on their culture.

Mike's experience at the DLI wasn't difficult for him. From his perspective, it was essentially being back in college full time except you were being **told** do so this time.

Those that were unmarried stayed in the barracks. JL was able to go home and see his family each day. My parents were provided field-grade housing in Monterey with 3 bedrooms and 3 bathrooms. They were lucky because some of their friends were assigned company-grade housing which only includes one bathroom.

My mom was very proud of her husband and bragged about it because of the difficulty to be accepted to the DLI. This was something I didn't appreciate at the time since I focused on my own 'problems.' My boyfriend, Carl, ended his active duty service with the Army in December and was going home to Wisconsin; so we decided to break up.

The Cross Country Adventure

The family left Fayetteville, NC in early December 1985 to head to California. The movers packed up the belongings from the house and the four of us somehow squeezed into Jean-Luc's pickup truck.

My sister and I sat in the bed of the truck (it had a top over it) with a mattress for cushioning. We also had Duke the hyper yellow lab riding in the bed of the truck.

That was a memorable trip, funny now, but wasn't at the time. One of the stops included a visit to Georgia to see my brother, John. I had to say goodbye to my boyfriend (Carl) in NC and then my brother in GA. That was very hard on me.

The truck was towing my mother's 1982 Toyota Supra. I begged them to let me drive the Supra instead of towing it and having to ride in the back of a pickup with my 12-year-old sister and the dog. The consistent answer was that we could get separated along the way. Maybe that was my intent...

Where was my car? I didn't have a car at the time because, well, I got into an accident prior to the move and the car was totaled - the Datsun B-210 car that Jean-Luc bought me after I graduated from high school.

My mom recalls that my sister and I kept to ourselves in the back of the pickup, we entertained each other through teasing and sometimes bickering. Apparently Jean-Luc had to re-establish some order a few times by telling us: "Please, behave and act like young ladies." That was one hell of a long cross-country ride in the back of a pick-up truck.

I was 20 years old, still poor and a fresh start in California sounded good. JL encouraged me to come along for the ride. But it didn't last long for me. Once I learned that they would be moving to Africa in two years and JL told me I should stay behind in the U.S., I made the choice to move back 'home' sooner rather than later.

My boyfriend, Carl, called on Christmas to let me know I was missed and invited me to visit him in Wisconsin to meet his family in January. I bought a one-way ticket and didn't tell him about the "one way" part. That's an important detail that I left out.

That's when I proceeded to tell my parents that I was leaving California. JL sat me down to have a conversation about leaving without any specific plans. He also said "you're young and *think* you're in love." While I appreciated his concern, that didn't stop me. I remember my mom was crying on the tarmac as I got on the airplane. JL was stoic and comforted her.

Carl was surprised when I arrived in Milwaukee with seven suitcases. He was speechless. He didn't have a job yet and was staying at his dad's until he got settled. I didn't even consider that he'd only been out of the military for about a month.

After visiting for a week, Carl drove me home to Georgia in his '69 Mustang so I could eventually get an apartment with my brother. We ran out of cash of course and Carl had to call his mother to send money via Western Union so he could drive back to Wisconsin. ATM's didn't exist back then.

I told my parents later that was "the plan" the whole time ... Carl would drive me back home to the South. (Not really, it just happened to work out that way).

After getting a job, saving money and buying my own car, I moved to Wisconsin in September 1986 and transferred to the University of Wisconsin after Carl proposed to me. My mom wasn't happy about my decision at the time—moving to Wisconsin—but being independent was a good decision for me.

About a year later, Carl and I flew to California to visit JL and my mom to celebrate our engagement. My brother, John, visited at the same time. My sister was happy to be with her siblings again.

We were able to fit in a trip to San Francisco with the whole family and got some beach time at Carmel-by-the-Sea, where Jean-Luc wore his famous American flag Speedo bathing suit. And it was famous.

For the Love of Skiing

My mom's civil service role allowed her to find employment at the Fort Ord Military Hospital fairly quickly. She was a counselor for abuses, marriage problems, adoptions and a discharge planner. As a discharge planner, every morning she did a round through the maternity ward, congratulating the new mothers and inquired if they needed help with the care of the newborns or any monetary assistance. Living in California is expensive compared to most of the U.S.

Military personnel on active duty are provided a family physician near their home. Captain Amy Ekstrom was their designated doctor. They struck up a friendship. My mom was also Amy's counselor since there were some issues with an ex-husband. During one of their conversations, my mom mentioned to Amy that she and JL like to snow ski. Amy wanted to learn and JL agreed to help and teach her.

I should back up a bit. JL also taught my mom to ski when they lived in NC. JL was a trained Special Forces skier and spent 3 years in Germany practicing that skill in the German Alps. He was an excellent skier obviously and wanted to teach my mom the sport he loved so much.

It was an arduous experience for my mom at first, she was clumsy on skis and was stubborn (her words), so it took some time for her to embrace skiing. One day it finally clicked and she was able to ski without falling and she started to like it.

She has one funny story from one of her earlier ski trips with JL. The slopes were very icy and as JL and my mom went down the slope, they made a left turn and encountered five female skiers sprawled on their sides. JL told my mom to wait on the side while he went to check and help those five ladies. After a few minutes of waiting, my mom decided she wanted to help too. The pass was very slippery and she couldn't stop before you know, skiing right over the five bodies. They were helpless.

My mom was very afraid that she'd fall before reaching the end of the pass, but made it. JL and the ladies were shocked at what just happened. No one was hurt thankfully. My mom yelled up to Jean-Luc "I went over five moguls and I didn't fall!" After that she retreated into the lodge to hide.

While living in Monterey, my mom went to Lake Tahoe as much as possible at the encouragement of JL. Every Friday there were organized ski trips through the Moral Welfare and Recreation of Fort Ord. The participants left at 5pm for Lake Tahoe and returned on Sunday at 5pm back to Fort Ord.

Jean-Luc couldn't attend the weekend trips often because of the studying demands required of him. Amy was on call a lot and her work schedule at the hospital was demanding. But they made it work out when possible.

Amy became my mom's ski partner when JL couldn't go. My mom became a self-described dare-devil sometimes on the slopes after the "5 mogul" experience. Amy was a beginner skier and my mom was average, yet they skied on slopes they shouldn't have been on sometimes.

When they were scared, they would yell "No Guts, No Glory" before descending down on a slope. Most of the time Amy would end up skiing on her bottom, but she never complained and never told my mom she was scared.

One morning they decided to try to ski the double back diamond slope, the main slope at Lake Tahoe, which is very steep and dangerous. Only the very skilled and advance skiers should do this slope but the "no guts, no glory" slogan convinced them it could be done.

The ski lift took them to the top of the slope and there they were – yikes! They yelled "No guts, no glory" and quickly realized it was a bad idea, the slope was extreme and beyond their skill level. My mom decided to walk down the slope instead of ski. Amy was behind her, up the slope, sitting down and crying for help because she was scared. My mom yelled back and said it was too steep for her to walk up and that she'd meet Amy at the bottom. Amy ended going down the slope on her bottom as usual.

My mom met up with Amy later and she was furious about what happened and wouldn't speak to my mom at first. They eventually made up later that evening and realized how lucky they were that neither were injured. JL wasn't on that weekend trip and he would have definitely discouraged attempting the main slope at Tahoe.

The Africa Tour

Being assigned to different U.S. Embassies sounds like a big party, with lots of events to attend and getting to meet important people from all over the world. But as an Attaché, Jean-Luc and the others were actually risking their lives each day to get information. His natural diplomacy skills often came into play in this position.

Sudan

After completing his training at the DLI in California, Jean-Luc graduated with a Master of Arts in National Security Affairs in 1987, and was assigned to Khartoum, Sudan to attend the General Staff College in Arabic, which is part of the U.S. Army Command. The Command and General Staff College (CGSC) develops officers to lead fighting units of the tactical and operational levels of war.

Jean-Luc's focus was on international Arab relations. His training was very intense because everything had to be done in Arabic while he was there.

Jean-Luc left California before my mother. He had her vehicle shipped to Sudan, then he drove cross-country again in his small pick-up; this time to his father's house in Connecticut. My mother stayed behind to supervise the household items that needed to be packed up and shipped to Sudan.

Since my mom didn't have a vehicle or a place to sleep, her supervisor allowed her to stay in her office at the Fort Ord hospital for a couple of days. A co-worker drove my mom and my sister to the airport for a flight to Washington, DC to connect with JL again.

Unfortunately, my mom and my sister had neglected to get their required shots for Africa before leaving California. JL had to take them to a clinic to get the immunizations, a slight unexpected delay in the journey.

My sister, Michele, had just started high school and there was not a school in Sudan she could attend as a military dependent. JL gave her 2 options: attend a boarding school in

England or Spain. She didn't feel comfortable at the time living in a country where she didn't speak the language. JL tried to "sell her" on Spain – that country was "rich in culture" and she would meet other teens from different parts of the world. Michele didn't really care at the time how rich in culture she could become. As a stubborn teenager, she would rather be poor in cultural experiences and not have to learn another language.

She decided on London Central, an American boarding school just outside of London for military dependents, and was located on a small U.S. Air Force Base in High Wycombe, England. My parents took her to London to get situated before they went to Sudan. It was almost a year later before my sister flew to Khartoum to visit them in Sudan.

Being away from Mom and JL was hard on her. The school offered a proxy family to help her cope. A "proxy family" brought students to their homes that had to stay in their dorms during holidays such as Thanksgiving and Christmas. JL also arranged and paid for Michele to join a couple of programs; one offered different field trips and one was a theatre tour group. She got to see a lot of beautiful tourist destinations and popular plays around England.

I was a college student in Wisconsin and wasn't really affected other than not being able to see the family or call them on the phone. Sending letters by international mail was our form of communication.

Since my mother had "spouse preference" distinction, she was able to get a position with the State Department as a Refugee Affairs Coordinators (RAC) at the U.S. Embassy. In the RAC office, they screened the Ethiopian and Eritrean applications for admittance to the United States as refugees. The applications were most often for people who suffered inhuman treatment under communist President Salas Salassi.

My mom was presented a drawer full of applications when she started. No one had done anything with the applications for a while and the sheer volume was overwhelming. That had to change. She set up a triage system where all the applications were read, checked and categorized into eligible or ineligible applicants. Computers were a new tool at the time and was very useful in that triage system.

While in Sudan, my parents were able to travel through North Africa and the Middle East. They took my sister to Morocco where my mother went to school as a young girl (my mother's father was in the French Army and stationed there after World War II).

In Egypt, they took a river cruise on the Nile and saw numerous tombs of famous Pharaohs. My mother said it was spectacular, however, it was in August and the heat was extreme. They visited the "City of the Dead" in Cairo, witnessing all the homeless people who live and work amongst the dead. They were fascinated by the locals, who cooked and dried their clothes on nearby tombs.

In Cairo, a man approached Jean-Luc and told him that his daughter, Michele, was beautiful and would like to marry her. He offered a dowry of 4 camels, 3 horses, 10 goats, etc. JL responded to the guy that Michele was worth a whole lot more than that, so he wasn't interested. The encounter was embarrassing for her to say the least.

My sister's first job was working at the U.S. Embassy's "post office" in Khartoum over the summer in 1988. My mom and JL worked during the day and she needed something to do, right? My sister was the only person assigned to work in the post office and that could be overwhelming sometimes, depending on the volume of mail that had to be sorted coming in and going out. And she only received one day of training.

The Marines that worked at the Embassy helped her out on occasion. Their locker room was next to the post office in the basement. JL made sure those young Marines knew Michele was only 15 years old and was off-limits. Their visits with her were to be strictly professional and no socializing with her. Looking back and as a parent of a girl now, my sister understands the potential "problem" of her being located in the basement of a building with a bunch of young guys.

During the Sudan assignment, Carl and I got married in 1988 and only my mother and Michele could attend, as JL couldn't take leave. The wedding was held in Appleton, Wisconsin, at a beautiful Catholic church. My brother John walked me down the aisle to give me away during the wedding ceremony. He was always my protector growing up.

When my mom and sister returned to Sudan, they were lucky the Khartoum airport was no longer closed. The Nile region received a record amount of rainfall while they were gone. The flooding even reached the basement post office, which was under several feet of water for a few weeks.

After two years in Sudan, Jean-Luc completed his General Staff College training. He made a speech entirely in Arabic at the graduation ceremony. My mom may not have understood a single word he said, but she was very proud of his accomplishments.

Psychological Operations (POG Airborne)

When his training in Sudan was complete, Jean-Luc was reassigned to Fort Bragg, North Carolina, in 1989. This meant my sister was able to come back to the U.S., and with two years left of high school, she could finish and graduate at an American school on American soil.

This also allowed JL to attend my brother's wedding to Sharon in 1989. I remember all the guys went out for the bachelor party the night before. The attendees included JL and my adopted father (my mom's second husband). This didn't seem to faze JL at all. Actually, I thought it was funny and took some pictures before they left as a group in several cars.

JL's new role was a Commander of a PSYOPS (Psychological Operations) Company, 3rd Battalion. PSYOPS are planned operations that channel selected information for targeted audiences to influence the emotions, motives and ultimately the behavior of individuals, groups, and organizations. These operations can take place during both peace and wartime.

JL was specifically part of the 4th Psychological Operations Group (POG) Airborne (A). The 4th POG (A) in Fort Bragg is the only active Army psychological operations unit now. It consists of 26 percent active U.S. Army operations units and the remaining 74 percent are reservists.

The mission of the 4th POG (A) is to be able to deploy on short notice, no matter their global location, and help to develop and conduct civil affairs and psychological operations to support the commanders, coalition forces, or other government agencies.

The soldiers and civilians that work as part of PSYOPS include regional experts that understand the political, cultural, and religious nuances of their target audience. Also included are experts in more technical fields such as broadcast journalism, radio, print, illustration, interrogation operations, and tactical communications.

These types of operations are also used to learn everything about the motivations of the targeted enemy—their beliefs, likes, dislikes, vulnerabilities, strengths, and weaknesses.

Then the Gulf War started in 1990.

Source: http://www.psywarrior.com/4thpog.html

Operation Desert Storm

"Our objectives are clear: Saddam Hussein's forces will leave Kuwait. The legitimate government of Kuwait will be restored to its rightful place, and Kuwait will once again be free."
~President George H.W. Bush

The first foreign crisis America saw following the Cold War occurred in August 1990 when Saddam Hussein ordered his powerful and large army into Kuwait. This was significant because of Kuwait's large oil supply, an abundance which was being supplied to the United States. It also jeopardized other countries nearby like Saudi Arabia who were big suppliers of oil and would allow Saddam to control roughly 20% of the world's oil.

President George H.W. Bush had a major role in Operation Desert Storm. When first confronted with conflict concerning foreign affairs and the possibility of the country's oil supply being put into the enemy's hands, the United States looked to him for his response. He said four short and powerful words: "This will not stand."

Saddam Hussein was essentially terrorizing the Middle East, especially Kuwait, with the desire to take over any country with power (in the form of oil supply for the most part) in order to make that power his own. The United States saw that international action needed to be taken and went to the United Nations Security Council to ask for assistance.

Iraq had been an ally of the Soviet Union and this worried Americans because the Soviet Union had the ability to veto any military action the United Nations presented. Thankfully, however, they did not veto the American's plan and the United Nations could begin the fight against terror.

The United States had roughly 500,000 troops stationed in Saudi Arabia to fight against Saddam. This was called Operation Desert Shield in the beginning.

President Bush gained support from the majority of Americans and a majority of Congress to go forward with their plan: warn Saddam Hussein that he had until January 16, 1991 to leave Kuwait or he would face the wrath of many countries in the United Nations. After waiting, Iraq gave no response and the next night Operation Desert Shield turned into Operation Desert Storm.

The operation began as bombings were dropped on Iraq's military targets for many weeks. On several days there were as many as 2500 missions being completed to destroy Iraq's military. Iraq then responded by sending Scud missiles to American military barracks in Saudi Arabia and Israel. The attack on Israel by Iraq was motivated by hopes that Israel's involvement would turn other nearby Arab nations to join Iraq. However, this failed as the countries remained opposed to Saddam and Iraq's motives.

After weeks of bombings, it only took 100 short hours for Kuwait to be declared liberated from the beginning to the end of the ground war. Iraq, still under Saddam's rule, stole millions of dollars from the occupying troops and set off bombs when traveling through Kuwait that then resulted in oil spilling into the Persian Gulf.

The casualties reported at the end of the operation were 148 Americans and an estimated 100,000 Iraqi deaths. This was considered a sign of strength for the United States and United Nations coming together militarily.

The United States passed its first test of a foreign crisis after the Cold War era had ended, and the largest military operation since Vietnam was considered a success at the time. Most Americans, for good reason, had faith and pride in their country and its military and technological advances in comparison with the rest of the world. President Bush stated at the operation's conclusion that: ***"New world order had begun."***

Sources:

http://www.ushistory.org/us/60a.asp

https://www.hoover.org/research/legacy-operation-desert-storm

http://www.twcenter.net/forums/showthread.php?676819-Schwarzkopf-s-Left-Hook-was-a-Miracle

http://www.psywarrior.com/HerbDStorm.html

Jean-Luc and his company, part of the 3rd Battalion, were deployed to Kuwait. JL was personally responsible for the safety of the Emir of Kuwait, Sheik Jaber al-Ahmed al-Sabab, during his time there. This was toward the end of the invasion in 1991.

My mother recalls JL telling her about all the fires in the oil fields. They couldn't see in front of them for several days because the smoke was so intense. While he was protecting the Emir of Kuwait, the soldiers that reported to JL went behind Iraq lines to do some reconnaissance. They brought back soil and sand samples, and other important intel. All those in his Company spoke and understood Arabic.

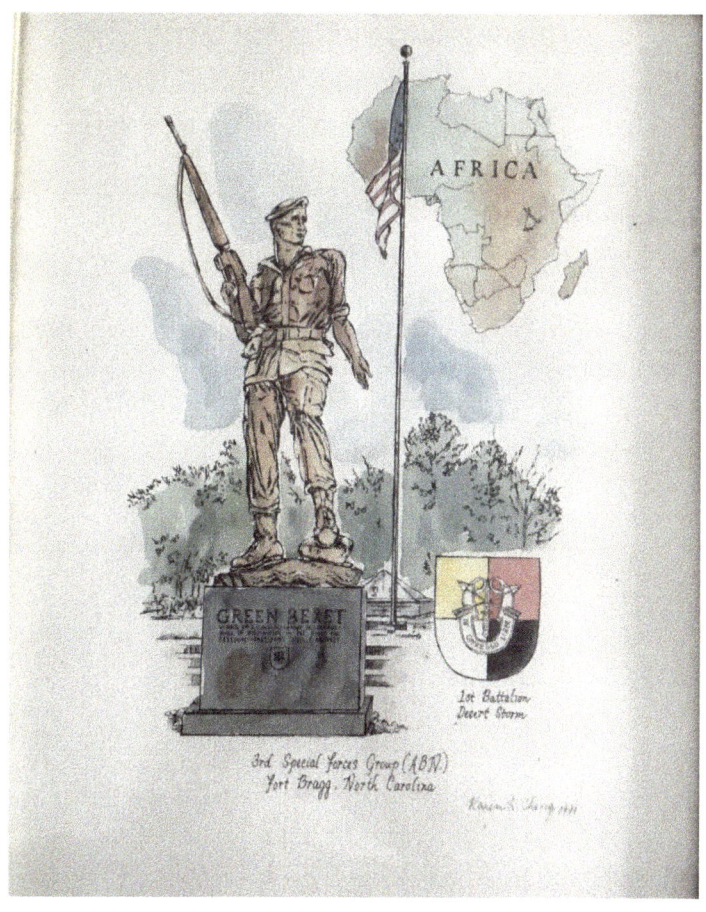

My mom and Jean-Luc were proud that Amy Ekstrom, the doctor they befriended at Fort Ord, was the first female soldier to enter Iraq. Amy was the company commander of a medic team during the first invasion of Iraq. Unfortunately, five of the medics that reported to her stepped on mines and died while trying to help some wounded soldiers.

The only other story about JL during Desert Storm I was able to glean was from the Benny's Wake after his funeral service. A meeting was called for all commanders and Jean-Luc was late for it. Everyone was seated already when he rushed in. As soon as he sat down, a grenade fell out of his gear and rolled across the floor slowly.

The grenade eventually rolled under the table where a general was seated. There was total silence that seemed to last forever. But it didn't explode, obviously. Jean-Luc was totally calm about it and retrieved the grenade from under the table after the meeting. There was loud laughter at the Benny's Wake after we all heard that story.

Life at home went on for my mom while he was in Kuwait. She did her best to support the spouses and the families of the soldiers. My mom encouraged the wives to send care packages to their husbands and to the single soldiers who didn't have anyone to send a care package.

My mom made several trips to the Commissary at Fort Bragg to purchase little items that might make their lives a little more pleasant ... such as decks of cards, crossword puzzles, magazines, note books, pencils, toothbrushes and toothpaste, deodorant, cookies, packs of gum, candy, etc.

She sent a senior enlisted man (he was a widow) practically the same thing she sent Jean-Luc. This guy later told her he really appreciated the extra attention.

While at Fort Bragg, she was offered a position with the Civil Affairs Company. My mom's experience with the Refugee Affairs in Sudan helped her get that role. The Enlisted Civil Affairs was a new component for the Reserved Army.

With the assistance of detailed enlisted NCO's (Non Commissioned Officer's) from the Reserve Army, she developed the Program of Instruction (POI) for the AIT (Advanced Individual Training), and developed the lesson plans.

At the same time, Jean-Luc challenged and encouraged my mom to finish her PhD. He kept pushing her in a positive way. This kept her busy. So during her breaks, lunch hour, any free moment actually, she continued to work on her dissertation.

The University accepted her dissertation and she received her Doctorate in Education with a specialty in psychology. The whole family was able to attend that graduation.

It's very interesting that they both were involved with psychology but from different aspects.

My sister was happy to be back at an American high school in Fayetteville, NC in this timeframe. Jean-Luc was gone for a total of three months in Kuwait and he returned just in time, safe and sound, for my sister's high school graduation in 1991.

A week before graduation, my sister had a car accident in the school parking lot. The damage was worth more than the car; a 1987 Pontiac Firebird and basically it was totaled. So JL bought her a 1984 Mustang convertible as a "graduation gift."

As a recent college graduate of the University of Wisconsin, I was offered a position in the Atlanta area. I accepted and we moved to the metro-Atlanta. This allowed my husband and I the ability to drive and attend her high school graduation in North Carolina.

My brother and his wife were able to attend as well. A lot was going on with everyone's 'blossoming' careers and it turned into a family reunion opportunity in May 1991.

We all stayed at our parents brick ranch house in Fayetteville for the weekend. Even though it seemed chaotic to us, you could tell that JL was very happy to be back home and embraced that chaos we brought.

Defense Attaché Course

Jean-Luc's secondary military specialty was as a Foreign Affairs Officer (FAO). In 1992, after three years at Fort Bragg, Jean-Luc received orders to attend the Defense Attaché Course at Bolling Air Force Base near D.C. He required additional training for future overseas assignments and this training would last a year.

My mom resigned her position as an Education Specialist in Fort Bragg and followed him to D.C. because they didn't want to separate while in the US. Plus my sister was a college student at that point.

The State Department and the Department of Defense were involved with the training and spouses were requested to attend training as well. Some classes were to be taken with the husbands and some were only for women, such as flower decorations, diplomatic etiquette, ribbon tying, etc.

Before attending the Defense Attaché Course, Jean-Luc had enrolled both my mother and himself with the "High Risk Defense Course" and the "Anti-terrorism Course." Those courses were given at Quantico, Virginia. My mom was surprised to have to attend those courses because Jean-Luc didn't tell her in advance. He was probably concerned that if she had a choice, she wouldn't attend. This training was needed because of their future assignments in Africa.

For the "High Risk Defense Course," there were 24 males, and one woman (my mom). The students were mostly agents working for the Federal Government, such as CIA, Secret Service, DEA, FBI, Defense Attaché, etc.

For the first four hours, my mom was pulled aside to receive individual training.

Staff Sergeant Green taught her how to shoot using muscle memory only.

My mom says she was nervous at first because she didn't want to embarrass her husband and was afraid of guns. She did as she was told, didn't complain, and actually enjoyed the experience. One of the exercises had her crawl on the ground while shooting; then had to jump out of a car window but the door was jammed so she didn't land gracefully. It was actually fun for her. And turns out she pretty was good at handling a gun.

One of the biggest tests had them all lined up in front of 25 silhouettes and each of them were given 25 bullets a piece. The mission was to put as many bullets into the targets as possible. The lights were turned off, it was pitch black, the signal was given, and they started shooting away. Using muscle memory, my mom concentrated on applying what she was taught. The lights came on, and instructors went to check how many bullets hit their targets. Two men missed completely their targets, and my mom and Jean-Luc both hit their targets 25 times.

The last test was a contest on who could shoot the fastest. They asked my mom to select her competitor, she chose Jean-Luc. At the given signal they began shooting, Jean-Luc went fast and tried to knock down the targets as fast as he could.

My mother went slowly, again applying what was learned about muscle memory, and concentrating on the targets. Her targets were falling, slowly yet surely, and she was catching up to Jean-Luc. All the instructors and other students were yelling "Go, go Michele, you are winning!" At the end she was declared the winner while JL insisted it was a tie.

She has never enjoyed a course as much as that one, and it helped her overcome that phobia of guns.

The next course, Anti-Terrorism, basically was called the "school of spying." My mom was not very good at it because she lacks one of the main ingredients – patience.

In one of the practical exercises, the main goal was to lose the person that was trailing you. They were provided some techniques to check if you were followed. One of the tactics was to look into a store window so you could see your surroundings without raising suspicions. The other one was to look into a small mirror like you were powdering your nose, mostly for women, and that was one of her preferred methods.

In one instance, my mom was being followed by an agent, she tried her best to lose him but he prevailed. She had so much "blush" on her face from looking into that small mirror, she felt like a clown. So she entered a department store and the agent was still behind her. She saw a bathroom sign, surely he was not going to follow her into the ladies restroom. She was near a women's clothing rack and dropped to her knees and tried to crawl to the restroom without being detected.

Unfortunately, a salesperson asked what she was doing crawling on the floor. She told the salesperson that one of her contacts fell out and she was looking for it. That worked. After 15 minutes, she emerged from the restroom after wiping the excess rouge from her face. No one was around and she rejoined the rendezvous place with a big smile.

She did not know who won that round but felt good overall because she succeeded in breaking her trail. That was the main goal.

The last exercise was a bit humiliating for her. The "class" was told that one of them will be under surveillance, that their mail and trash can would be searched.

Jean-Luc and my mom were confident that no CIA agent would come to their residence because it was more than a two hour drive from the school. They even discussed that the agents probably would need TDY (temporary duty assignment) orders to search their garbage can because it was too far.

On the last day of training, the instructors showed them a movie about their surveillance. The movie showed a woman wearing an old shabby bathrobe, house slippers and loose socks, curlers in her hair. She looked like a poor pitiful housewife.

Their classmates were giggling seeing that poor lady on the screen. After a few seconds my mom realized that woman was HER. She was so embarrassed that she crawled under the desk and did not come up until they stopped the film.

My mom's conclusion – CIA agents are sneaky and they know how to do their job. She's fairly certain they use this example to future students as an example of what "Not to Do" if you are under surveillance. It was a humbling experience.

Chad

Before my parents left for Chad, I remember Jean-Luc specifically telling me that if something bad happened to them while they were gone overseas, not to tell the media who my parents were. It would put us in danger.

Turns out a previous Defense Attaché in Chad was killed in Paris by an Islamic terrorist. A lot of Europeans were targeted as well.

When Jean-Luc was the US Army Defense Attaché in N'Djamena, Chad, there were several unrests with the population. One evening JL received a call from the Marines that there was a kidnapping of a U.S. civilian and his Chadian spouse. In a situation like this, the RSO (Regional Security Officer) gets involved and is supposed to assist the assigned Marines.

The RSO didn't respond. So Jean-Luc didn't hesitate after receiving the call for help. He jumped into the Defense Attaché SUV and decided to intervene to help the couple. After a few hours of negotiation with the kidnappers, Jean-Luc obtained the release of the couple.

Another incident at the Marines' Ball at the U.S. Embassy is worth telling. While everybody was dancing, eating, drinking and being merry, Jean-Luc learned that their next door neighbor in Chad was shot during a carjacking. As usual Jean-Luc did not hesitate, jumped into the SUV and went to investigate the shooting.

My mom was left alone on the dance floor, no partner, no way home. The American community had a good time listening to their verbal exchanges on the radios that night.

Radios were used as their main form of communication. Satellite phones or land lines were not an option. The radios were secure but did not allow for privacy if others are around.

Being outspoken, impatient and feisty, my mom has a tendency to entertain. (As her children, we know this to be true.) Jean-Luc's radio handling was "North Pole," my mom's was "Tampa."

One example: "North Pole, this is Tampa, I am lost, can't find my way home."

"Tampa, can tell me where you are?"

"North Pole, if I knew where I was I wouldn't be lost, right?"

Another time, their pet "AK", a little aggressive desert deer (they believe it was mistreated by some Chadian guards) attacked one of the guards on their property. My mom was at home and provided first aid to the guard. AK put a huge hole into the guard's leg, my mom said she nearly fainted when she saw the wound.

AK was excited by the commotion and decided to try and gore my mom's leg. She jumped on a nearby bench and that quick reaction saved her leg. Angry and frustrated, she called Jean-Luc on the radio. He was at the U.S. Embassy when she called.

"North Pole, this is Tampa, I want you to know that AK gored one of the guard's leg. The wound is so deep you can see the bone, and AK tried to put a hole in my leg too. If you don't come home right away, I will get my pistol and shoot that pest." She heard laughter from the radio after her burst of anger.

While Jean-Luc was in Chad, he was informed of President Carter's visit to the country. JL was assigned to provide the safety of the President and his entourage. Since President Carter was scheduled to meet the President of Chad, Jean-Luc requested and obtained permission to assess the safety of the palace. He thoroughly inspected and interviewed the security guards, then he informed the U.S. Ambassador that it was safe for President Carter.

The reason for President Carter's visit was to introduce health education and medicine to the country of Chad on behalf of the Carter Center. The specific medicine was to help prevent and cure Guinea Worm disease, which is a parasitic infection from drinking stagnant water and was prevalent in Chad. This medicine is also used to prevent River Blindness, which is caused by black flies that are infected with parasites; those flies can bite humans and cause blindness.

My mom with President and Mrs. Carter at the U.S. Embassy
(picture taken by JL)

Remember the gun training my mom received prior to JL's assignment in Chad? She's thankful for that because it came in handy. There were two instances when their house in Chad was broken into even though they had assigned guards for the property. Jean-Luc was not at home either time.

Mom specifically remembers one instance when she woke up from the alarm system blasting in the middle of the night. She grabbed the Glock on her nightstand, the AK-47 from the closet, then went downstairs to shut the alarm system off and proceeded to search the house. The door leading to the terrace was half way open, so she closed and locked it. She speculates that the intruder (or would-be thief) saw the weapons she was carrying and ran away.

Most people would be terrified in that situation, she wasn't at the time, and it took a few months later for her to realize the danger she was in. The instructors apparently did a good job training her for moments like that; and she was ready to apply what she learned—"shoot first and ask questions later."

The terrace was located at the back of the villa and could only be accessed with a ladder. Why did those two incidents happen when her husband was out of town and why was the terrace door unlocked and opened?

In the morning, my mom confronted the cook because she suspected he was "in" on this and left the terrace back door unlocked on purpose. He denied it. She didn't fire him because of the effort to get another cook, and he was a good one, especially with crepes suzettes. She felt "safer" after the conversation and knowing that her friends, the AK-47 and Glock, would protect her.

Luckily, no other break-ins happened after that during the remainder of their stay in Chad. She added that break-ins happened frequently there and foreigners were robbed of jewelry and money, especially when someone was away from their home.

While JL was still assigned to Chad, a war broke out in Rwanda. There were two rival tribes that were committing genocide; the Hutus were killing the Tutsis and vice versa. Thousands of bodies were found everywhere. The French Army came in to intervene, the U.S. sent some soldiers, so Jean-Luc and a few other U.S. Defense Attachés were sent to assist.

JL was the liaison between the French Joint Task Force and the U.S. Joint Task Force. They were there to provide humanitarian assistance. Bodies were floating in the river... typhus, black plague, and typhoid fever broke out in the refugee camps. It was a calamity. The epidemic killed 2,500 Rwandan refugees daily. (This stat came from JL's resume.)

Jean-Luc was saddened by so much evil and cruelty within those tribes and he felt helpless at times witnessing so much misery.

Back "home" again

After the Chad assignment completed, they returned to the U.S. in 1995 and Jean-Luc was assigned to Ft Meade, MD. My mom was reinstated into Civil Service and was assigned to the Walter Reed Hospital, Washington, DC, as a Research Psychologist.

Jean-Luc retired from the military after 21 years (in 1996) and upon retirement, he received the Legion of Merit award. This is a higher level than the Bronze Star for Valor. What's impressive is that he was Major at retirement and that award is usually given to higher ranking officers.

He then had the opportunity to work overseas as a security consultant, mostly for Exxon and other oil companies. He worked in the Republic of Congo, Cameroon, Niger, Nigeria, and Turkmenistan, just to name a few.

His role was to secure the work sites, keeping the equipment and crew safe. The average time away was 6 months at a time, some events were 12 months and some were 3 months. Those travels inspired him to bring back hand-made gifts for everyone in the family from the countries he visited. On one trip he bought a special hand-made necklace for each of the seven different grandchildren.

The pay as a consultant was excellent but the separation was burdensome on their marriage. My mom's position in Washington, D.C. had her travel a lot too and she was able to travel a few times to Africa to be with Jean-Luc on his international assignments. A lot of those countries spoke French, she is fluent in that language and felt at home anywhere she went.

The Civilian Life

The transition to civilian life after service was fairly easy. Jean-Luc was part of a strong community and connected with the right people. They looked beyond the soldier and saw leadership, empathy and problem solving skills. You can adapt better to an environment when your normal has been moving around a lot. Jean-Luc was definitely accustomed to that.

The Grandpa Role

When not traveling abroad in his role as an international security consultant, JL installed himself as a leader with the grandchildren...Grandpa. He was a wise sage and gave out the best advice. JL actually knew how to connect with any child, not just his grandchildren.

I took this picture of JL with all the grandsons at my brother's house in 2003 after JL returned from one of his 6-month gigs in Africa.

Being a grandparent brought Jean-Luc so much joy and he wanted to spend as much time with them as possible.

One of his favorite things to do was *literally* dress up as Santa Claus when he came to visit at Christmas time. This started when he was on active duty, toward the end of his military service. The role of Santa Claus was important to JL. He would ask each of the grandkids if they've been good and what they wanted for Christmas. Santa brought gifts only to well-behaved children. All the boys believed it.

When my younger son was around 8 years old, he set-up a video camera, pointed it toward the fireplace and wanted evidence of Santa leaving gifts. The set-up didn't capture any footage of Santa coming down the chimney that night and he was disappointed. The kids eventually figured it out the connection between Grandpa and Santa.

We visited my parents a couple times in the DC area. We were able to fit in visits between JL's international consulting assignments. JL took my family on a tour of DC during spring break once. My sons were 4 and 7 years old at the time. The boys had a great time exploring with Grandpa, seeing the wonderful monuments, eating great food, and celebrating my sons' April birthdays.

My sons with Grandpa during one of his personal D.C. tours

My brother, his wife Sharon, and their sons visited our parents in DC a couple of times too. On one of their summer trips to DC, his oldest son, Eric, had to go to the emergency room on their visit. He bit his tongue while playing in the playground with Grandpa. There was a lot of blood everywhere apparently. Without going into detail, this injury required stitches on Eric's tongue. That was painful, but it's funny now.

He also had nicknames for the middle grandsons to make them feel stronger: Jake the Snake, Ryan the Lion, and Dylan the Villain. All three had older brothers to deal with.

JL took Brent, the first grandchild, on one of the first big international trips with a grandchild. JL and my mom traveled to New Zealand and Australia with Brent for 3 weeks, the summer before he started 2nd grade.

That first trip overseas set a high expectation for the other grandchildren. All of them experienced out of the country trips with Grandpa eventually. Their favorite trips were going on a cruise with him, which was simpler overall and less intense for everyone.

The only granddaughter, Alexis, was able to go on one of the fanciest trips. She went on a month-long trip to Europe that included a cruise to Greece and Italy in 2015. The rest of the trip was visiting my mom's relatives in France. I remember JL using Skype on that trip so Alexis could speak with her mom (my sister) and her Aunt Brigitte.

9-11

We all remember what we were doing on that day. And each of us has a unique story. My parents were living in Alexandria, VA. I was in Chicago attending a big trade show and had been there already for 10 days, away from my family.

Everyone was watching the news on TV that day. There was mayhem everywhere and horrible pictures of the New York Towers collapsing. Over and over, they were showing pictures of people jumping from the windows to avoid being burned to death. Again, I was in Chicago and we were instructed to stay away from sky-rises and to hang out at the trade center. The trade center showed the news on the big projector – the screen size was probably 30 times bigger than a standard TV.

When I learned about the Pentagon being hit, I tried to call my mother. We were very concerned because we knew she had meetings at the Pentagon and prayed she wasn't there on that day. I couldn't reach her or Jean-Luc; this was before she had a cell phone. Cell phone coverage was spotty everywhere on that day by the way. JL eventually called our house and spoke with my husband to let him know they were okay, and that my mom was out of town at a conference.

I was stuck in Chicago for another 3 days with my coworkers and we were able to get a rental bus back to Atlanta. All rental cars were taken. By the time the bus arrived "home," it had been 13 days since I had seen my husband and 2 young sons. This made me question where I put my focus.

On September 9, 2001, my mom traveled to San Diego for a research conference representing the US Army, since she was one of their Research Psychologists. She arrived at the hotel around 5:00 PM Pacific Time, and was able to get a room at one of the bungalows near the conference room. Mrs. Maude, the wife of a lieutenant general, was attending the conference as well.

Monday was a very busy day and my mom attended as many presentations as she could, and took good notes for her office coworkers. On Tuesday morning – 9/11 - about 6:00 AM (Pacific Time, 3 hours behind Washington, DC), Jean-Luc called her hotel room to tell her that an airplane plowed into the Pentagon. The five floors where the airplane entered had collapsed and there were several deaths and injuries.

She immediately turned on the TV. Mom couldn't believe her eyes when she saw the Pentagon on fire and smoking, with a huge gap in the middle of it. To most people, the Pentagon was impenetrable and the strongest building in the world.

Exactly one week before, she was inside the Pentagon attending a meeting in the conference room, the same one, where so many were trapped and died. Crying, shivering and confused, she decided to get dressed and go outside for some air. As soon as she reached for the doorknob, the phone rang; it was Mrs. Maude calling for help. Mom responded that she was on the way.

My mom immediately dialed the room of one of the social workers attending the conference and then she contacted her office back in D.C. She was ordered to watch the general's wife very closely due to shock.

My mom assured the supervisor that she would do her best. Christine (a co-worker) went with my mom to Mrs. Maude's room to keep her company.

The general's wife was very calm and composed, she didn't believe that her husband was killed. Mrs. Maude told Christine and my mom that her husband was somewhere in the Pentagon building, perhaps in a restroom unconscious.

Denial is a typical reaction to a traumatic event. Mrs. Maude asked my mom to call the D.C. office to be sure that they checked everywhere for her husband. My mom complied and called the office to convey her request.

They were told that the police and rescue personnel checked throughout the building; however, they didn't find any trace of him and they feared that he may have been one of the first to be killed. They spent the biggest part of the day watching the Pentagon building and Mrs. Maude continually pointing out that the exterior windows of her husband's office did not appear to have suffered from smoke damage.

My mom focused on distracting the general's wife, to include getting lunch for the three of them. Later that day, the general's wife was able to get a seat on a VIP plane to Washington, DC.

Christine and my mom stayed behind and tried twice daily to book a flight back to Washington. They were finally able to get a red-eye flight back home on Sunday morning, 5 days later, and Jean-Luc was able to pick her up at 3:45 AM. He was definitely happy to have her back home.

My mom returned to work the next morning. Since she was the last one to be scheduled, she was slotted to work from noon to 8:00pm. The US Army used the Sheraton to conduct business, such as counseling to families of victims, information center, and feed-back to inquiries.

There were daily briefings and a high ranking general provided information that was not provided to the general public. He explained to my mom and others how they identified the bodies or what was left of them. The floors were covered with several inches of debris and ashes, the debris and ashes were gathered and spread out on tarmacs in parking lots. Cadaver dogs sniffed through the ashes, and bone fragments were gathered and DNA tested. This was how most of the victims were identified.

DNA from family members were taken and matched with the DNA of the bone fragments. She believes two victims were never found, it was assumed that they were dissolved from the infernal heat. One of the families wrote a congressional complaint because they were unable to identify their son.

Tragedies like these bring out the best or the worst in people. Security was very strict, you couldn't enter the Sheraton unless you had a badge. However, if you were a victim's family member you could have access through the door, where a roster of names could be checked.

One afternoon, a lady came in and claimed that she was the President of the United States. One of the guards very calmly asked her to wait and made a sign to another guard to check with security.

Two policemen came next to her and the woman became very agitated and asked "Why are there two policemen accompanying me?" The police officer's response was, "You are the President of the United States. We want to secure your safety; it is our job, Ma'am!" Very proudly she exited the hotel with the two policemen escorting her to a patrol car and back to the hospital where she came from.

There was another incident where a woman claimed that her nephew was killed in the Pentagon. They checked the name that she gave and there was no match. Later on, she returned with a wig, different clothing, different name, no luck, nor match.

According to witnesses, this woman did the same thing five times. As a psychologist, my mom didn't know if she was unbalanced or just curious. She didn't have the chance to talk with that persistent woman, but it was entertaining to everyone at the time.

Within three weeks of 9/11 happening, JL had to leave for a 5 month trip. This time the destination was to Turkmenistan, which is just north of Iran and Afghanistan. His resume lists that he was deployed to Turkmenistan on an "emergency basis" to provide security for three different locations there.

This is what his resume states regarding the Turkmenistan assignment:

"Conducted security assessments; liaison with host-country national security agency and international organizations; developed mail-handling procedures to deal with any possible threats; updated the evacuation plan; performed vehicular reconnaissance of the overland evacuation route to Kazakstan; added an emergency charter aircraft capability, and added a standby boat capability.

Plotted geographic coordinates for all critical locations and routes. Had 10 vehicle Global Positioning Systems (GPS) installed; programmed all GPS's, and conducted GPS training. Helped coordinate aviation support; established a VHF communications system; oversaw well-site physical security enhancements; established and coordinated a 41-man guard force; and designed and installed a video/intercom system to control office access."

Being alone was hard on my mother after dealing with the recent trauma of the 9-11 Pentagon victims and their families. I remember talking to her a lot on the phone and we all were worried about JL.

He never shared what he was dealing with.

Florida: The final destination

The international assignments that JL accepted were tough on my mother while they lived in Alexandria, Virginia; there was no family near her. She was thankful to be working, which kept her busy and she would visit JL overseas when it was allowed.

This went on for 3 more years and then my mom finally retired from Civil Service. We saw my parents a lot more once they moved to Florida because of the closer proximity to Georgia, where my siblings and I live.

Jean-Luc and my mom moved to Florida in September 2004, near NAS (the Naval Air Station) by Pensacola just in time for Hurricane Ivan to hit.

They literally moved into their new home two days after closing on an old horse farm, and were waiting for their furniture to be delivered when the hurricane hit the 5-acre property. Eighty trees were knocked down while my mom and JL were hunkered down in the basement.

The area didn't have water or electricity for two weeks, the majority of roads were flooded and they had to eat MRE's (Meals Ready to Eat). My mom is actually thankful JL had MRE's available. It's amazing their house or the 6-stall horse barn wasn't damaged or flooded.

Jean-Luc allowed neighbors to drive through their property to have access to a main road that wasn't underwater. A big section of the property fence had to be removed for this to happen. The neighbors were very grateful to him.

Jean-Luc joked that his new home was like Green Acres.

After their move to Florida, we all started hanging out with JL more, which was his goal. Such wonderful memories for the grandkids - beach trips and horse camps every summer. One summer he made it a point to take all 6 of the grandsons to Disney World at the same time. He and my mom were outnumbered – the age of the grandkids were 3 years old (Dylan) up to 12. The only granddaughter wasn't born yet.

The grandsons and JL played a lot of games on his property. One of their favorite things to do was play hide-and-seek with Grandpa. In most cases, Grandpa would win because he used techniques that would blend him in with the background. All the boys declared that Grandpa was cheating because he was trained as a spy.

On one Spring break visit, my sister's family arrived and JL started playing baseball with Brent, who was 12 years old at the time. My sister and her husband were in the house unpacking. JL came inside within 30 minutes and had his hand over his eye to cover the bleeding and bruising.

My sister asked what happened. JL had been hit by the baseball – this was from him pitching the ball and Brent hit the baseball with a bat.

My mom was teaching at the local college, she is still a part-time French teacher, so my brother-in-law took JL to the emergency room. There was a high risk of JL losing his sight, he couldn't lay down for over a month and had to sleep upright in the recliner so that the retina wouldn't detach. JL had to also wear an eye-patch for a while; he made the most of it and pretended he was a pirate.

JL reassured Brent that it wasn't his fault, it wasn't a big deal, and it was just an accident. He was always good about telling everyone not to turn things into a big deal. Stuff happens.

Grandpa also liked to give financial advice. He wanted to teach the value of money to the grandkids especially and the importance of saving. I have a lot of emails from him regarding that subject.

One of the great things JL did for his grandchildren was the idea to open a mutual fund account with $10,000 after each were born, which ended up being 7 different accounts. The money would be accessible to each of them on their 22nd birthdays. My mother actually made it happen because Jean-Luc was in Africa on different assignments when each grandchild was born.

As previously mentioned, JL stayed in contact with Harry Shaw. He was there with Harry in 2010 when Harry participated in a skydiving event in Texas on the 27th anniversary of Harry's injury from Grenada. It required special equipment for Harry to participate because he lost both legs up to his hips.

I watched the interview video of Harry's commemorative skydive, noticed that JL quickly got out of way after landing and didn't want to be recorded. He wanted Harry to be the focus, as it should.

Jean-Luc after the skydive jump in Texas with Harry in 2010

Jean-Luc with Harry Shaw and Don Mooney in Houston after JL's oldest grandson (Brent) graduated from military training in Texas in 2013.

A few years after my parents moved to their property, a stray Mini Pin (miniature Doberman pinscher) without a collar showed up on the property. Jean-Luc went around and asked the neighbors if anyone knew who owned the dog. He even put up signs, placed an ad in the local paper and called the animal shelter. No one claimed the dog.

The dog was tiny, literally was about 8 pounds, and JL decided to name him Rocco. He claimed that little Rocco adopted him and not the other way around. Rocco had a Napoleonic complex according to JL, the dog was always by his side, and JL gave Rocco the nicknames "bonehead" and "little guy."

Rocco escaped the property all the time. Six years later on one of his adventures, he snuck into another fenced property and got into a fight with a much larger dog. Rocco's lung was punctured. JL was sad to lose this little guy.

After Rocco was buried, JL laid on floor in front of the TV and my mom saw tears running down his cheeks. She asked if he was crying and he denied it. His response was that big men don't cry.

Jean-Luc emailed this pic to us after Rocco's death

Jean-Luc had this marker made and placed over where Rocco is buried.

JL traveled a lot to his grandson's sports events. He always kept his calendar up-to-date with the specific locations, times, the sport (mostly baseball games) and which grandchild. My younger son played travel ice hockey and that was a challenge for Grandpa to see those; he made it happen a few times.

Jacob had the opportunity to play in a hockey tournament at the Air Force Academy. It was a great experience and he proceeded to tell Grandpa that he wanted to play hockey for the Air Force. With raised eyebrows, Grandpa's response was, "Are you sure? West Point is a better option."

Brent joined the Army after graduating from high school. JL was proud of that and made sure he attended every military training graduation ceremony for Brent. One of them was jump-school graduation in Fort Benning. Brent became a paratrooper just like Grandpa.

He also enjoyed taking videos and pictures of the family get-togethers and shared with all of us via email. Grandpa became the family documentarian. His camera was always nearby and we are thankful he captured all those moments.

My mom and Jean-Luc celebrated their 30th wedding anniversary in 2012 with an Eastern European trip to include Russia and a cruise. She has always wanted to visit Moscow and he made sure that happened. And of course, he had his camera with him and took pictures of the beautiful architecture that Moscow is known for.

JL was able to attend his 40th West Point graduation at West Point in October 2015, about 5 months before he passed away. He was so happy to connect with his fellow cadets on campus again. This is when he created a Facebook profile to connect online with everyone.

Recreation of the D-4 Yearbook picture from 1975 – 40th reunion, 2015

One of the last things JL did was visit my brother's family. Ryan had a baseball game and Grandpa was there to watch; it was on his calendar, so you know it was important to him. My brother's other son, Eric, called when the baseball game was over and explained to my brother that his vehicle wouldn't start.

JL heard the news, immediately changed his plans, and decided to stay longer to help my brother figure out why the car wouldn't start. He told my mom, "my grandson needs my help and I can't leave until we figure this out."

The next weekend he passed away. The family's "normal "took a major detour.

We later saw that Jean-Luc had hand-written on his calendar the upcoming high school graduation dates for two of the grandsons – my son, Jacob, and my brother's son, Ryan. He died two months before those graduations. It was hard on them that Grandpa wouldn't be there in person.

He's with us in spirit now. This is something that provides comfort; knowing the positive impact he made with so many.

My nephew, Eric, wanted to share his speech that he gave at the funeral.

A Grandson's Tribute

Thank you all for coming today. It means a lot to see all the people that care and loved my grandpa. He did many great things in his life and being our grandpa was one of those, and I believe one of his favorite things.

Like my other 6 cousins, some of my best memories are with him. From all the trips together we went on and all the games he came to, thank you for all the memories. I will cherish them forever.

He taught me and my fellow grandchildren many things that are now instilled in our character - like don't be wasteful (by making us eat our food), treat women with respect (by holding the door open and let girls go first) and always find the best in a situation.

On December 11 this past year, it was my grandparent's 33rd anniversary and it was the day before my own wedding. And without hesitation or a thought, they both came to my rehearsal dinner. This is just one of the many examples of how my grandpa would put his grandkids in front of himself. But that was just the kind of person that he was, someone that gave much more than he ever took.

I implore everyone to try to be just half the person my grandpa was. And if that happened, the world would not only be a better place, it would be a place I would be happy to raise my daughter in. My daughter, who is 18 months old right now, will never get the chance to get to know him, but I will always tell stories about how great he was and how much he loved her too.

The one thing I will miss the most is whenever I saw him, he said these two words that were followed by a big hug, "Hey Grandson" and I will miss him saying that to me forever.

Proverbs 3:5 and Proverbs 3:6 - (5) Trust in the LORD with all your heart and lean not on your own understanding; (6) in all your ways submit to him and he will make your path straight. We are not meant to understand what God's planning for us, but we must trust it is the best for our wellbeing and our loved ones.

Grandpa, you will always be missed more than anyone will know. But I know you are in a better place and we will see each other again.

Love you always,
Your Grandson, Eric

Epilogue

Life goes on and we continue to move forward. My mother has surrounded herself with good friends and continues to stay active. We've all had to visit the property multiple times since JL's death and help out with various projects because 5-acres needs constant attention.

Mom is slowly going through his things and donated his uniforms to the University of West Florida. The University plans to place his uniforms in their museum along with some of his other military items. It is an honor for this to happen.

After sifting around his stuff, we learned that Jean-Luc received numerous awards while on active duty. This guy was a bad-ass. Most people would have those awards displayed on their office wall or something.

Here's a list of the military awards by precedence he received:

- Legion of Merit
- Bronze Star for Valor
- Bronze Star for Achievement
- Defense Meritorious Service Medal
- Meritorious Service Medal
- Joint Service Commendation Medal
- Army Commendation
- Plus numerous campaign service ribbons

My mom also found some letters (folded in envelopes) on his desk next to his computer with each grandchild's name handwritten on the envelope. She handed out each respective letter the day after the funeral. Each envelope also included a unique necklace from Niger.

We all found these letters comforting. It was his usual way of handing out advice, mixing in some history. He was all about personal development. Even after death.

As I was going through my notes for the book, I wanted to share at least one of those letters and chose the letter he wrote to my youngest son, Jacob. Ironically, the letters (they're not dated) to each grandchild were written a week before his death according to my mother.

Did he have a sense death was going to happen soon for him?

Letter to a Grandson

Jake,

We finally found the Tuareg necklaces that I bought in Niger five years ago for each one of you grandchildren. Grandma hid them (too well) so I could give them to you for Christmas 2011. Each of the necklaces are in the form of a unique cross that represents one of the 21 oases in the Tuareg region.

The Tuareg are Berbers who live across the Sahara desert in northern Africa. They are nomads who plied the great camel caravan routes and are known as determined and fierce fighters. They are usually armed and, if you are unarmed, it is normally not a good idea to cross paths in the desert.

The men, from the age of 25, begin wearing a veil (cheche) which conceals their entire face except for their eyes. They also wear long robes to protect them from the desert. The Tuaregs are sometimes referred to as the "Blue People" because their traditional cheche and robes are died with an indigo pigment which stained their skins a dark blue. While Tuaregs are mostly Muslim, their women are not veiled like the men. Some Berbers are blonde and blue eyes, and there are some who believe that is due to Viking raiders in the past.

I selected the Iferouane cross for you. Iferouane is an oasis town near Arlit in northern Niger and is located in the Agadez region deep in Tuareg territory. I worked several times in Niger as a security consultant and manager. I put many miles driving a Toyota Landcruiser in the Sahara desert and was often the only westerner for 500km or so.

I planned, scouted, selected and marked routes through the dunes and from our logistical base in N'Guigmi to our oil exploration sites and provided security for a 360km move of an oil derrick and supporting equipment and personnel. It would take about 130 truck sorties to move all the needed equipment.

supporting equipment and personnel. It would take about 130 truck sorties to move all the needed equipment.

When working for oil companies, I had to visit Agadez on numerous occasions to coordinate with the regional military commander reference the 98 Nigerian soldiers assigned to us to provide our security. I am familiar with Iferouane because it is the location of an Areva (French nuclear power company) uranium mine. I did a security assessment for a company providing 54 ton dump trucks to Areva and visited Iferouane, Arlit, and all of the small villages in the area.

I had to study and assess the security threats and learned a lot about the Tuaregs. They're a fascinating ethnic group. Tuaregs are great artisans and specialize in silver jewelry, leather artifacts, and finely crafted swords and daggers.

Your necklace does not look factory perfect because it is handmade by a Tuareg nomad. Tuaregs consider gold a demonic metal, which is why they make their jewelry out of silver, the metal of Allah. The crosses provide a mix of religious and superstitious protection. They provide the protection of God, but they are also thought to provide the protection of beneficial genies who protect you from the evil eye and from the evil Jinn spirits.

Tuareg crosses were passed down from fathers to sons with the words, "My son, I give you the four corners of the world, because one can never know where one will die."

Grandson, I give you the four corners of the world.

Love,
Grandpa

Final thoughts

Unknowingly we emulate those around us. We tend not to notice the value or influence of others until we see the world through their particular lens or when they are gone.

What people like Jean-Luc do is essential to protecting our country. Their efforts allows people like you and me to create, write, pursue our interests (whatever they are), and have the opportunity to make something of ourselves. He was a true patriot and warrior.

Family was everything to him. After my conversations with Keith Huber, it made me realize that those in the military need their family more than we can imagine. We gave JL that needed 'normalcy' and we inspired him as well.

The best thing a father can do for his children is to love their mother. That's exactly what Jean-Luc did for 33 years. We never questioned his devotion. His death reminds us to hug your loved ones each day. Hold them tight and tell them how much you love them.

Thank you Jean-Luc for making a positive impact and being a great role model for our country, your community, and our family. Thank you for inspiring us all to improve ourselves, not be afraid to try new things, make time to explore, and have the courage to do what's right at any given moment.

And most of all, thank you for loving our mother.

~Brigitte

Acknowledgements

This book would not have happened without the help from so many people. It was definitely a group effort.

Keith Huber, Dan Alexander, Joseph Wasiak, Stan Moore, Don Mooney, Harry Shaw, Tim Andruss. All of you knew JL while on active duty, and were generous with your time and input. You guys made this book a reality.

Thank you for your generosity Zachary Willey and providing the personal West Point tour. You didn't even know me beforehand or my stepdad, but helped out because you're part of The Long Gray Line.

My mom was a big supporter of the book idea and shared a lot of stories. This strengthened our bond even more.

My husband, Carl, supported me the most; and his steady and patient personality came in handy. If you've ever written a book, you understand the need for balance at home.

It was fun looking back at the shared experiences with my sister, Michele, and my brother, John. We viewed it from a different perspective now that we're older. Michele also helped with editing. Thank you for sharing your speech Eric.

I appreciate Mike Ray sharing his experience at the DLI and it was great to catch up with my high school friend! Devan Barker provided the research on the Grenada invasion and Desert Storm.

Patrick Lewis and LeRoi Cochran kept me on track with the book and provided some needed altMBA-style feedback.

And thank you to Tracy Stalling and Megan Copenhaver.

www.ingramcontent.com/pod-product-compliance
Lightning Source LLC
Chambersburg PA
CBHW040324300426
44112CB00021B/2872